Preston Parrish knows what it
eloquent book, he shows glimp
again the wonder and glory of
on whose faithfulness we can always depend.

R. Albert Mohler, Jr.
President, The Southern Baptist
Theological Seminary, Louisville, KY

Preston Parrish has been my good friend for more than 30 years, and we've had
many opportunities to work together in proclaiming the life-changing gospel of
Jesus Christ around the world. His new book, *Windows into the Heart of God*, shares
biblical insights into the Person of Jesus that help us see Him as God and Man,
Servant and Savior, King of kings and Lord of lords. The book's 31 chapters invite
us to draw near to Christ and to let each encounter transform us for His glory.

Franklin Graham
President and CEO, Billy Graham Evangelistic Association
President and CEO, Samaritan's Purse

This book could have been called *Glorious Glimpses of God*. It is more than "windows";
it is a magnifying glass on the life of the Master. Indeed, it is a life-transforming
look at the One who said, "I am…the life. None comes to the Father but by Me."
Every Christian needs these spiritual snapshots of their Savior.

Dr. Norman L. Geisler
Former President, Southern Evangelical Seminary

Glimpse the heart of God through the impact of the Word of God on Preston
Parrish's heart. Preston displays truth about the God we know in Jesus Christ in
language that is biblical and yet creative and even fun. His own heart is open wide
as he displays the effects of the heart of God and the life and work of Jesus Christ
in his own life. Your heart will be touched, too, as you see the impact of God's heart
and the truths of His Word on the heart of another.

Robert C. (Ric) Cannada, Jr.
Chancellor and CEO, Reformed Theological Seminary

Peering out of windows often allows us to see reality that otherwise would be
walled off. In *Windows into the Heart of God*, Preston Parrish gives us a glimpse
of Jesus through the windows of our common life experiences. No longer are we
walled off from the reality of God's presence and love. His book is inspiring and
transforming!

Mark Earley
President and CEO, Prison Fellowship Ministries

Windows
into the HEART *of*
God

HARVEST HOUSE PUBLISHERS

EUGENE, OREGON

Cover by Abris, Veneta, Oregon

Cover photo © Creatas Images / Jupiterimages

WINDOWS INTO THE HEART OF GOD
Copyright © 2007 by Preston Parrish
Published by Harvest House Publishers
Eugene, Oregon 97402
www.harvesthousepublishers.com

Library of Congress Cataloging-in-Publication Date
Parrish, Preston, 1955-
Windows into the heart of God / Preston Parrish.
   p. cm.
ISBN-13: 978-0-7369-1954-8 (pbk.)
ISBN-10: 0-7369-1954-6 (pbk.)
1. Spirituality—Meditations. I. Title
BV4501.3.P3725 2007
248.4—dc22
                                                        2007002505

Printed in the United States of America

07 08 09 10 11 12 13 14 15 / LB-SK / 12 11 10 9 8 7 6 5 4 3 2 1

To Glenda—
the wife of my youth,
whose life is a glimpse of Jesus

Acknowledgments

At this time I want to express my thanks for...

Bruce and Virginia Parrish, the loving parents that God, in His perfect wisdom, gave me;

Larry Heath, a faithful servant Christ used to introduce me to Himself when I was a searching teenager;

Turk and Eleanor Peverall, in-laws who graciously welcomed into their family the young man marrying their only daughter;

Franklin and Jane Graham, friends and witnesses for the gospel through all the thick-and-thin the years have dished out;

Billy and Ruth Graham, true examples of Christian evangelism who befriended Glenda and me when we were newlyweds;

David Burr, Gene Witmer, Roy Gustafson, Ann Willis, Charlie Tope, Dick Capin, and other elders who encouraged and taught me so much;

Jeff and Jodie Chetwood, friends who've loved our children as their own;

Alan and Ann Wright, friends in ministry who get to enjoy the beach more than we do;

Mel and Terri Graham, friends whose tender hearts are worth more than gold;

Loran and Sandra Livingston, friends who give so much of themselves in ministry without expecting anything in return;

Steve and Jeanne Scholle, friends and colaborers who brought our son-in-law Max into the world;

Judy Green, Dana Vines, and Beth Decherd, friends who—along with other families and the staff of Charlotte Christian School—have blessed me by blessing my wife and younger daughter with much kindness;

The Kids' Club (not really kids anymore)—you know who you are—you greatly enrich our lives;

Christian radio stations that broadcast the good news of Jesus Christ in word and music, especially these fine stations in the region where we live: WMIT 106.9 FM, based in Asheville, North Carolina; WBFJ 89.3 FM, based in Winston-Salem, North Carolina; and WRCM 91.9 FM, based in Charlotte, North Carolina;

all our partners, supporters, and helpers in the work of the gospel along the way, including Paula Woodring, Shelley Erickson, Nancy Chatterton, and the rest of the staffs of the Billy Graham Evangelistic Association, Samaritan's Purse, and *AWAKENINGS*—

The LORD bless you and keep you;
the LORD make His face shine on you, and be gracious to you;
the LORD lift up His countenance on you, and give you peace
(Numbers 6:24-26).

Contents

About the Title

Deliberating with the publishers of this book to develop its title was an exercise in opinions—theirs, based on their considerable expertise and understanding of how books are best presented to potential readers, and mine, based on...well, based on my opinion!

In the end, however, we came to a title that seemed appropriate to us all:

WINDOWS into the Heart of God:
31 Life-Changing Glimpses of Jesus

Windows intrigues me because the Bible speaks of the "windows of heaven" (Malachi 3:10), which God promises to open to those who rightly honor Him with their resources. While that oft-quoted portion of Scripture is certainly true, windows can also have another application. In addition to being a picture of how blessings come *from* God, windows can also enable us to see *into* something or, in this case, Someone. Perhaps that was part of the reason why the Old Testament prophet Daniel, languishing in exile in Babylon, prayed three times daily with his "windows open toward Jerusalem" (Daniel 6:10). Yes, he was longing to return to that beloved city. Even more, however, he was seeking greater insight into the heart of God.

Speaking of *the heart of God,* the Scripture records that God Himself commended David as "a man after His own heart"

(1 Samuel 13:14). Enough said about that phrase—that's the highest aspiration any of us can have.

As for *glimpses,* Job declared in the midst of his suffering, "If I go to the east, he is not there; if I go to the west, I do not find him. When he is at work in the north, I do not see him; when he turns to the south, I catch no glimpse of him. But he knows the way that I take; when he has tested me, I will come forth as gold" (Job 23:8-10 NIV).

As you'll see in this book, we know something about suffering…about straining to catch a glimpse of God in the midst of it…and about striving to survive and pass His tests and to come forth as gold refined by fire. Because of Jesus, doing just that is possible for each of us as we trust Him and depend upon His grace and mercy.

So…I'm happy to embrace my publisher's preference for this book's title. Actually, it was my idea all along—I'll just let them take the credit for it. (Yeah…right!) And I hope reading *Windows into the Heart of God: 31 Life-Changing Glimpses of Jesus* blesses you as much as having the opportunity to write it has blessed me. Thanks, Harvest House.

Preston Parrish
Charlotte, NC

Introduction

He fascinates me.

Actually, that's an understatement. The person of Jesus Christ utterly captivates me, and He has done so ever since I placed my faith in Him well over three decades ago.

My interest in Him is not mere curiosity or casual interest. Nor do I view Him from the perspective of an academic studying some figure in history (though history is calculated around His appearance). I don't focus on Him as one might scrutinize the life of some noted author or artist, some inventor or scientist or mathematician, some military, political, or religious leader, in order to understand his accomplishments.

I worship and serve Him as God.

Is that true for you as well? Perhaps you want to, but don't know how. You may wonder what all the Jesus hubbub is about and whether there's any relevance, meaning, or hope for you in Him. Or you may already believe in Him but want to know Him better.

The point of this book, quite simply, is to help you draw near and be transformed by Him. My aim is not to reveal some "newly discovered" titillating story giving the "inside scoop" on the "real" Jesus. Rather, my desire is to relate insights into His nature and work that come from the one and only Book that's reliably all about Him: the Bible. These are insights I'd want to share with you if we were able to enjoy a cup of coffee by the fire or relax on the patio with a glass of iced tea…insights that will truly deepen your experience of Him. And, at the same time, I want to do what I can to dispel some of the shallow and, at times, downright ridiculous caricatures of Him floating around today.

I want to say up front that, in addition to coming from the Scriptures, these glimpses of Christ also flow through the prism of my own life (but in my defense, what human communication *doesn't* flow through somebody's life?). This admittedly presents a problem. That's because my life, at its worst, can horribly distort and obscure the light of His glory. In fact, on my own, I'm just plain darkness.

At its best, however, my life (and yours) can display at least some of the manifold richness of Christ's beauty. All the brilliance, warmth, and power of the sun—all the colors, patterns, and textures of the world around us—these pale in comparison to the love, grace, and truth found in Him, which can increasingly mark our lives as we lose ourselves (or more accurately, find ourselves) in Him.

Moving from the worst to the best—that's the challenge. During the course of my life, I've learned something about this challenge: It hinges on our relationship with Him.

Apart from Him, even our highest achievements and most resounding successes fall short and ring hollow. With Him, however, even a life that appears quite ordinary can flourish with a quality and fullness that are, well, heavenly.

And, as you'll see in this book, this can be the case not only on days when, both literally and figuratively, the sun is shining and the birds are singing, but also on days when rain and thunderbolts crash from the clouds with heart-melting ferocity.

So here's a story of Jesus—31 "windows," if you will, into the One who is Himself the very expression and embodiment of God's heart.

The Bible says, "Draw near to God and He will draw near to you" (James 4:8). It also says, "...beholding as in a mirror the glory of the Lord, [we] are being transformed into the same image" (2 Corinthians 2:18).

Draw near to Him...get to know Him...be transformed by Him.

I think you'll find, as I have, that your glimpses will more and more become a gaze that never lets you go.

Part One

Before He Came

*He was foreknown before
the foundation of the world...*

1 Peter 1:20

Begotten

*The Word became flesh, and dwelt among us,
and we saw His glory, glory as of the only begotten
from the Father, full of grace and truth.*

Jesus didn't just weep and laugh *like* a real
Son—He *was* (and is) God's real Son.

A piece of wood that wept and laughed like a child.

That's how writer Carlo Collodi described the origins of his fabled character Pinocchio back in 1881, when he wrote his children's classic. In case the details of the story are a bit dim in your memory, "a common block of firewood" that would come to have uncommon characteristics wound up in the possession of a "dapper little old man" named Geppetto.

"I thought of making myself a beautiful wooden Marionette," Geppetto said. "It must be wonderful, one that will be able to dance, fence, and turn somersaults. With it I intend to go around the world, to earn my crust of bread and cup of wine."

Thus, Pinocchio came into being. Throughout the story, however, Pinocchio repeatedly rebels against and disappoints his "parent."

Most notably, his nose grows longer every time he tells a lie. Despite his unusual abilities, the wooden doll is continually frustrated that he isn't like other boys. By the final chapter, however, he learns to be virtuous, and a fairy rewards him by making him a human being. The story ends with Pinocchio exclaiming, "How ridiculous I was as a Marionette! And how happy I am, now that I have become a real boy!"

Foundational in drawing near to Christ and being transformed by Him is realizing that He is begotten. What does the term "begotten" mean? It speaks of the relationship between a parent and child, and it indicates that the child genuinely comes from the parent.

Glenda and I married while we were in college, and God subsequently blessed us with four children—Hannah (whose birthday is the day before mine, who qualifies as our family "drama queen" and has keen insight into people), Gregory (actually my namesake, who was hearty even before birth and loves physical and practical challenges), Nathan (born with a disposition to "enjoy the journey," yet with a quiet determination evident from the outset), and JesseRuth (who has what I call "million-dollar" eyes and an electric smile, with an extraordinarily kind heart). Each one genuinely came from us, and I could not deny it if I wanted (I don't!).

For some wives and husbands, though, having a child that is biologically their own flesh and blood is an unfulfilled longing. Experts say that infertility affects about 10 percent of the reproductive-age population. Many couples dealing with infertility spend thousands of dollars to overcome it. Some never do have the joy of welcoming into the world one of those bundles of humanity that can cause so much upheaval! (Thankfully, some couples choose to adopt, resulting in great blessing for those "chosen" children and for themselves.)

To attempt to compensate for their childlessness, couples could construct a "being"—even one that walks, talks, and expresses some semblance of emotion—from silicon chips and other materials. The product, however, would nonetheless be just some*thing* they made, not some*one* begotten by them who shares their nature and genetic code. (In fact, our kids had a toy robot like this some time ago. It became such a nuisance that we were glad when it finally broke!)

Jesus, however, really is God's unique Son. God Himself bore witness to this fact, announcing from the heavens when Christ was baptized in the Jordan River, "This is My beloved Son, in whom I am well-pleased" (Matthew 3:17).

The Lord Jesus Christ said it too, speaking of Himself when He said, "For God so loved the world, that He gave His only begotten Son, that whoever believes in Him shall not perish, but have eternal life" (John 3:16).

It was a desire to state this truth clearly that compelled church leaders in the fourth and fifth centuries to declare in the historic statement of belief known as the Nicene Creed: "We believe in one Lord, Jesus Christ, the only Son of God, eternally begotten of the Father, God from God, Light from Light, true God from true God, begotten, not made, of one Being with the Father..."

This side of heaven, our finite minds won't be able to comprehend fully the mystery that Christ is God's begotten. Yet we *can* grasp that Christ is one of a kind and has no peer. One commentator said it this way: "Jesus is all that God is, and He alone is this."[1]

Christ's stature as the only begotten Son of God was not confined to His earthly life. He was already the Father's Son before the Father sent Him. The apostle John wrote, "By this the love of God was manifested in us, that God has sent His only begotten Son into the world so that we might live through Him" (1 John 4:9).

I don't mean to be irreverent, but this raises a logical question: If Christ was already the Son of God before He came into the world, what were He and the Father doing then?

Right now, we can't know all that was taking place in their relationship before Christ appeared on earth. But the Scriptures do clue us in to some things. In fact, all we have to do is eavesdrop as, on the night before His death, Jesus lifted up this prayer for His followers:

I glorified You on the earth, having accomplished the work which You have given Me to do. Now, Father, glorify Me together with Yourself, with the glory which I had with You before the world was.... As You sent Me into the world, I also have sent them into the world.... I do not ask on behalf of these alone, but for those also who believe in Me through their word; that they may all be one; even as You, Father, are in Me and I in You.... that they may be one, just as We are one; I in them and You in Me, that they may be perfected in unity, so that the world may know that You sent Me, and loved them, even as You have loved Me.... Father, I desire that they also, whom You have given Me, be with Me where I am, so that they may see My glory which You have given Me, for You loved Me before the foundation of the world (John 17:4-5,18,20-24).

Notice some of His themes?

- Their perfect unity...
- Their shared purpose...
- Their common glory...
- Their everlasting love...

The picture begins to come into focus at least a little more.

I'm especially intrigued by Christ's references to glory. Israel's great liberator, Moses, once prayed, "Show me Your glory!" (Exodus 33:18).[2] God's glory has been defined as the sum of all His goodness. In the Scriptures, God's glory repeatedly appears as shining, brilliant radiance. I'm often reminded of God's glory when I see fireworks exploding in the night sky, illuminating everything around with breathtaking beauty and power. (In fact, at this very moment, I'm watching such a display from the window of a hotel room near a popular theme park.) The constant, undiminished glory between the Father and the Son before the Son came into the world—along with their love, oneness, and common purpose to impart eternal life to fallen people—had to be a concentration of goodness that was something of infinite beauty and power. (Thankfully, as we'll see later, it continues even now.)

And that glory was evident, at least in some measure, as His sandal-shod feet walked the dusty roads of the Middle East: "The Word became flesh, and dwelt among us, and we saw His glory, glory as of the only begotten from the Father, full of grace and truth" (John 1:14).

In his book *Knowing God,* James I. Packer wrote that God's fatherly relationship with Jesus implies four things: First, it implies authority; second, it implies affection; third, fellowship; fourth, honor. "God wills to exalt his Son," he says.[3]

Authority, affection, fellowship, and honor—these don't occur with "a common block of firewood" or any other manufactured thing. They can only take place in a relationship with one who is of the same nature. And because Christ is God's only begotten Son, He alone is authoritatively able to reveal God to us:

> No one has seen God at any time; the only begotten God who is in the bosom of the Father, He has explained Him (John 1:18).

It is in His face alone that "the light of the knowledge of the glory of God" definitively shines (see 2 Corinthians 4:6). Only Jesus is altogether pleasing to His Father. Only Jesus is ample for the work vested solely with Him: saving people separated from God by their sins. Millions of adherents to idolatrous religions across the globe—who, in the words of the Old Testament prophet Isaiah, "fall down before a block of wood" (Isaiah 44:20)—would spare themselves a lot of time, effort, money, and anguish if they would just recognize this truth.

Millions more who consider themselves too sophisticated to worship idols of wood or stone would find peace and freedom if they would stop trying to save themselves or earn their way to heaven—if they would cease looking to earn "a crust of bread and cup of wine" for their hungry, parched souls—through worldly works and possessions, and instead, simply depend on Him.

On the night before He was crucified on a Roman cross, Jesus took bread, gave thanks and broke it, saying to His disciples, " 'This is My body which is given for you; do this in remembrance of Me.' And in the same way He took the cup after they had eaten, saying, 'This cup which is poured out for you is the new covenant in My blood' " (Luke 22:19-20).

The One doing this was God's only begotten Son. Jesus didn't just weep and laugh *like* a real Son—He *was* (and is) God's real Son. And He gave His body and blood so that whoever chooses to turn from their sins and place their faith in Him will know here and now, as well as forever, the joy of His fellowship.

DRAW NEAR AND BE TRANSFORMED

Our temporal well-being and our eternal destiny depend on our response to God's only begotten Son, the Lord Jesus Christ, in whom He delights: "He who believes in Him is not judged; he who does not believe has been judged already, because he has not believed in the name of the only begotten Son of God" (John 3:18).

The good news is that any friend of the Son is welcomed by the Father. Have you determined to count on Christ alone for forgiveness and acceptance by God? If not, you can do so right now. Just call out to Him and ask Him to be your own personal Savior. He said, "The one who comes to Me I will certainly not cast out" (John 6:37).

If you've already taken this step, pause right now to reaffirm your faith and express your gratitude that the One who is God's real, unique, one-of-a-kind, peerless, fully pleasing, only begotten Son loves YOU...then let that realization infuse your soul afresh with heavenly peace and joy.

2

I will surely tell of the decree of the LORD:
He said to Me, "You are My Son, today I have
begotten You. Ask of Me, and I will surely give the
nations as Your inheritance, and the very
ends of the earth as Your possession."

PSALM 2:7-8

Jesus' delight was to do His Father's will.
His Father's delight was to establish Him as
the heir and ruler of all things.

Candlelight cast a warm glow through the cavernous stone chamber. Reflections of the flickering flames danced in the eyes of the select group assembled there. Now and then, a jewel would sparkle, punctuating the anticipation in the air.

The year was 1804.

The place: the cathedral Notre Dame de Paris.

The occasion: the coronation of Napoleon as emperor of France.

For this historic event Napoleon, consistent with his renowned ego, was going about things his own way. Writing about his political and military views, he once wrote in a letter to his brother, "Since one must choose sides, one might as well choose the side that is victorious, the side which devastates, loots, and burns. Considering the alternative, it is better to eat than be eaten." He also once declared, apparently without the slightest bit of hesitation or embarrassment, "I am no ordinary man." Perhaps the clearest summary of his outlook was his bald assertion, "Circumstances—I make circumstances!"

Now, for his coronation, Napoleon was conducting himself accordingly. Refusing to travel to Rome to be crowned by the pope as his predecessors had in predominantly Catholic France, he instead summoned Pope Pius VII to Paris. When the pope arrived, Napoleon did not kneel before him or kiss his hand, considered the traditional demonstrations of humility. He was determined that his authority would be self-derived and that he would owe it to no one.

In a supreme act of audacity, when the time came for him to kneel before the pope and receive the crown, Napoleon—dressed in his red coronation robe and carrying his scepter—reportedly stepped toward the altar, seized the crown, and put it on his own head![4]

What a contrast with the King of kings and Lord of lords, Jesus Christ, who seized nothing for Himself and delighted to receive everything from His heavenly Father. This was true of Christ before He came to this earth, and it was true while He was here. It was true of Jesus' words; it was true of His works; it was true of His authority. Jesus said and did nothing independently of His Father, nor did He Himself strive for position and prominence.

To the contrary, Christ's preeminence was decreed by His Father long before He came into this world. His delight was to do His Father's will, and His Father's delight was to establish Him as the heir and ruler of all things. When Jesus did appear, this proved to be a point of stumbling for many whom He encountered.

One day, for example, some Jews were contending with Jesus. Refusing to be bound by their traditions, He was saying and doing things that put them in a bad light. In particular, Jesus healed a man on the Sabbath:

For this reason the Jews were persecuting Jesus, because He was doing these things on the Sabbath. But He answered them, "My Father is working until now, and I Myself am working."

For this reason therefore the Jews were seeking all the more to kill Him, because He not only was breaking the Sabbath, but also was calling God His own Father, making Himself equal with God (John 5:16-18).

Wow! Talk about a mouthful! But Jesus didn't stop there. Consider these statements by Him:

- "Just as the Father has life in Himself, even so He gave to the Son also to have life in Himself; and He gave Him authority to execute judgment, because He is the Son of Man.... I can do nothing on My own initiative. As I hear, I judge; and My judgment is just, because I do not seek My own will, but the will of Him who sent Me" (John 5:26-27,30).
- "I and the Father are one" (John 10:30).
- "He who has seen Me has seen the Father.... Do you not believe that I am in the Father, and the Father is in Me? The words that I say to you I do not speak on My own initiative, but the Father abiding in Me does His works" (John 14:9-10).
- "This is eternal life, that they may know You, the only true God, and Jesus Christ whom You have sent" (John 17:3).

Far from being the words of some stereotypical "gentle Jesus, meek and mild" who was campaigning for the popular vote and attempting to cheer and please everybody, these declarations drew a line in the Middle Eastern sand on which Jesus and His hearers stood. It was a line drawn by God Himself and it extends throughout time and eternity. On one side are those who recognize and worship Christ for who He is—God's only begotten Son—and on the other side are those who refuse to do so. As the apostle Paul wrote:

> He is the image of the invisible God, the firstborn of all creation….all things have been created through Him and for Him. He is before all things, and in Him all things hold together…. He Himself will come to have first place in everything (Colossians 1:15-18).

Scripture also says, "The Father loves the Son and has given all things into His hand. He who believes in the Son has eternal life; but he who does not obey the Son will not see life, but the wrath of God abides on him" (John 3:35-36).

Yet even in His supremacy, Jesus looks for allegiance and obedience that is born of love for Him, rather than grudging submission. His invitation to come and follow Him is still a gracious one—one that has transformed the lives of multitudes who have trusted Him. Even the bombastic Napoleon acknowledged this, at least in some measure:

> I know men, and I tell you that Jesus Christ is no mere man. Between him and every other person in the world there is no possible term of comparison. Alexander, Caesar, Charlemagne, and I have founded empires. But upon what did we rest the creations of our genius? Upon force. Jesus Christ founded his empire upon love; and at this hour millions of men would die for him.

Before the beginning of time, God decreed that His Son would reign over everything. Whether or not we agree with Him doesn't affect that decision (it does have consequences). But God, in His kindness, also determined that He would give us the opportunity to embrace His Son willingly. Bringing this to pass, however, involved a plan that was…well, astounding. This plan was foretold through the centuries.

DRAW NEAR AND BE TRANSFORMED

Have you ever considered that God, being God, could put into place a plan that does not depend on your agreement for its success?

How do you respond to the biblical assertion that Jesus Christ will come to have first place in everything?

Have you willingly embraced Christ as God's appointed heir and ruler, or have you resisted doing so thus far?

Have you considered the implications of persisting in a course of thought and action that differs from God's?

What could be more important than declaring your allegiance to Christ, who is not only loved by His heavenly Father but who also loves you today?

foretold

A child will be born to us,
a son will be given to us.

Isaiah 9:6

God planned and is executing the mission
of His Son with absolute precision.

Waves crashing on the beach are one of my favorite sounds. In fact, for most of my life, the ocean is where I've gone to find physical and mental refreshment. It's the place where, since Glenda and I were dating in high school, we have soaked up the sun, gazed for hours at moonlight shimmering on the water, and watched spellbound as on countless early mornings and late afternoons the divine Artist mixed colors with unending variety and splashed them across His celestial palette.

It's also the place where we've shared some of our most memorable times with our children. I remember Hannah, when she was a toddler, running terrified for her life from sea gulls that seemed bigger than she was. I remember Gregory feverishly digging a hole in the sand that eventually became so large it swallowed him from view (*Why is he working so hard on vacation?* I wondered). I remember Nathan, barely tall enough to hold a fishing pole, declaring that he was going to catch a flounder…and much to everyone's surprise, doing so. I remember JesseRuth with an expression of sheer delight on her face as rushing water washed back and forth over her tiny toes.

The ocean is also the place where I've had lots of adventure— once, for example, windsurfing far beyond where the shrimp boats troll, till from land I was just a speck on a watery horizon, only to have the late afternoon wind die. With darkness approaching I had no choice but to jump into the water and paddle my way back to shore through clusters of sea turtles, jellyfish, and sharks (well, there could have been—after all, while fishing we've caught sharks longer than six feet well within sight of swimmers!). When I finally dragged myself exhausted onto the beach, alarmed police officers, rescue workers, and vacationers—not to mention my family—were all searching for me. Because I made landfall some distance from where I set out, it took a while for people to notice that I was very much present and alive. I couldn't tell whether they were more relieved or annoyed!

Whatever my experience during my various visits to the beach, one constant I've come to expect is the tide—rising and falling, surging and receding, not once but in two complete cycles daily. I'm always amazed by the predictability of the tide. High tide and low tide occur with a faithfulness that is charted, published, and counted on by vacationers, surfers, fishermen, and mariners across the globe. You can even buy "clocks" that show you the current status of the tides.

While tide charts appear to be a simple schedule—much like one you'd receive for a bus or train—they are actually complex calculations requiring careful consideration of numerous factors, including astronomical, topographical, and historical data. While occasionally some seismic activity beneath the ocean will create a rogue wave, tidal predictions have a very small margin of error and are, for practical purposes, quite reliable—more so, for example, than weather forecasts.

Not long ago while driving on the highway I saw a billboard promoting the superiority of a local television station's weather forecasts over those of their competitors. "It's not that they're wronger," said the ad. "It's just that we're righter."

When it comes to the mission of God's only begotten Son, it's not a matter of being "wronger" or "righter." In fact, there is no margin for error. God planned it and is executing it with absolute precision. He even foretold it in startling detail. This mission begins unfolding in the earliest chapters of the Bible.

In Genesis, for example, God had spoken into being the physical realm. You may be saying, "Wait a minute! Stop right there! That's an assertion I'm not ready to accept." Allow me, however, to start where the Bible starts: "In the beginning God created the heavens and the earth" (Genesis 1:1).

Permit me also to point out that, while there is a considerable body of scientific evidence supporting this declaration and a significant number of respected scientists who espouse it, you and I both must ultimately approach it not with a test tube but with trust.[5] In fact, the Bible itself says, "By faith we understand that the worlds were prepared by the word of God, so that what is seen was not made out of things which are visible" (Hebrews 11:3).

If this causes you to stumble, let me suggest this: Albert Einstein himself once indicated that, by his reckoning, he knew less than two percent of all that there is to know. Even if you and I are as brilliant as Einstein (I'm not raising my hand!), it is certainly possible that the proof of God's creative work resides in the 98 percent of knowledge that we do not now possess. It would be the height of folly—or, dare I say it, arrogance—to dismiss the Bible just because we don't presently see how what it says can actually be. There are too many examples in history, archaeology, and other disciplines, of biblical assertions that were once deemed preposterous but subsequently proven correct. And in this case, the stakes are high—indeed, ultimate.

We owe it to ourselves to consider Christ fully and honestly as

He is presented in the Scriptures. After all, because God is God and could hide from us forever if He chose, the only way we can know Him is through whatever revelation of Himself He chooses to give us.

As one person in Scripture queried: "Can you discover the depths of God? Can you discover the limits of the Almighty?" (Job 11:7). Another answered: "The Almighty—we cannot find Him" (Job 37:23).

Revealing Himself definitively and authoritatively, however, is precisely what God purposed to do by sending His Son into the world. Jesus Himself said, "No one knows the Son except the Father; nor does anyone know the Father except the Son, and anyone to whom the Son wills to reveal Him" (Matthew 11:27). And the Son's appearance is an event that God chose to foretell, bit by bit, beginning with the first man and the first woman, Adam and Eve.

The background against which God began to unfold His plan is important. Adam and Eve, having been placed by God in a garden where they lacked for nothing and enjoyed perfect fellowship with Him, chose to go their own way and disobeyed the one command God had given them: "The LORD God commanded the man, saying, 'From any tree of the garden you may eat freely; but from the tree of the knowledge of good and evil you shall not eat, for in the day that you eat from it you will surely die'" (Genesis 2:16-17).

They chose instead, however, to grab for what God, in His love and wisdom, had withheld. They ate of the fruit of that tree. "Then," the Bible says, "the eyes of both of them were opened, and they knew that they were naked; and they sewed fig leaves together and made themselves loin coverings" (Genesis 3:7).

What followed next was a sorrowful scene in which God pronounced the punishment for Adam and Eve's disobedience, which included pain and toil and, as He had forewarned them, death. They were banished from the Garden of Eden to live out their days bereft of the blessings God made them to enjoy—not, however, before God Himself gave them a merciful promise and performed a gracious act.

In Genesis 3:15 God promised that a "seed" of the woman would "bruise" (or in some Bible translations, "crush") the head of the tempter, embodied as a serpent, which had beckoned them to rebel. What's the significance of that?

Well, as I was driving into our office this morning, a copperhead snake—a species of poisonous snake that especially loves the wooded areas here in North Carolina—lay stretched across the road. Workers were grouped around it (a clue to me that the snake might not still be alive!). Pausing to look at it myself, I saw that a car had apparently run over the snake's head and "bruised" it—in fact, it was crushed flat. It was indeed dead; never again would it inflict pain or instill fear in anyone.

By declaring that the serpent's head would be bruised, God was promising Adam and Eve—as well as every person born after them—that one of their descendants would inflict a fatal blow on the tempter and put an end to his power. That's why Scripture later says, "The God of peace will soon crush Satan under your feet" (Romans 16:20).

Then, in Genesis 3:21, God went on to make "garments of skin for Adam and his wife, and clothed them," replacing with something more lasting the flimsy coverings they had stitched together for themselves.

Here, in this dark setting of ruin and loss, God was already beginning to reveal His plan for rescue and redemption—for salvation from sin and its consequences—that would eventually be carried out by His only begotten Son. It's likely, however, that on the ground there in the garden was a hint of what it would cost: blood. The animal whose skin clothed Adam and Eve provided their covering at the ultimate price—the price of its life. The cost to the Son of God for bruising the serpent's head and dealing with human sin would be nothing less.

This truth, and so much more about Him, was progressively fore-told and recorded in Scripture in ever-sharpening detail as successive generations of descendants of Adam and Eve were born, lived, and died. Events through the centuries pointed to Him as well.

Consider, for example:

- God's rescue from the great flood of His faithful servant Noah, along with his family, in an ark that some archae-ologists believe now rests ice-encased on Mount Ararat in modern-day Turkey. In the New Testament this event is cited as a picture of salvation, in which only those who trust in Christ avoid destruction;

- God's blessings and promises in the life of the Old Tes-tament patriarch Abraham, all of which hinged on Abraham's faith. The New Testament makes clear that we are saved by God's grace "through faith" in Christ (Ephesians 2:8);

- God's deliverance from bondage in Egypt of the nation descended from Abraham, his son Isaac, and his grand-son Jacob, who was also called Israel. Only those who sought refuge under the blood of the Passover lamb escaped death and exited to freedom under Moses' leadership. The New Testament presents Christ as the Passover Lamb sacrificed for us.

Perhaps one of the clearest prophecies (*prophecy* has been defined as history written in advance) of the coming and work of God's Son was spoken by the Jewish prophet Isaiah around 700 B.C. He declared:

A child will be born to us, a son will be given to us; and the government will rest on His shoulders; and His name will be called Wonderful Counselor, Mighty God, Eternal Father, Prince of Peace. There will be no end to the increase of His government or of peace.... The zeal of the LORD of hosts will accomplish this (Isaiah 9:6-7).

The many prophecies about the fact that the Son would come, the manner of His coming, the place of His coming, the response to His coming, and the outcome of His coming, when taken together as a whole, all sharpened into focus to create a statistical improbability of such enormous magnitude that no one except God's Son could actually fulfill them. As time passed, the question on many minds was whether it would really happen—or, to say it another way, would the tide of God's salvation arrive as anticipated?

DRAW NEAR AND BE TRANSFORMED

Have you concluded that the only things that can be true are the ones you presently understand, or are you allowing for the possibility that God's work and ways are larger than the limitations of your finite mind? Defend your conclusion.

How do you respond to the idea that, because God is greater than we are, our experience of Him depends on what He chooses to reveal to us of Himself rather than what we can "research" about Him?

How do you respond to the assertion that Jesus Christ is God's definitive and authoritative revelation of Himself?

Have you ever considered that God, who perfectly planned the mission of His Son, also has a plan for your life? What difference would living by His plan rather than by your own, or even by none at all, make in your circumstances and outlook?

4

Anticipated

Oh that I knew where I might find Him,
That I might come to His seat!

JOB 23:3

God's plan was to come to the hurting
human race and take His seat here.

Hell was in session.

At least that's the way one person who endured the ghoulish experience described it. And the release of its survivors and their reunion with their families marks one of the most memorable episodes of anticipation in American history.

The time was the latter half of the 1960s and the early years of the 1970s. The United States was embroiled in a military conflict in Southeast Asia that was rending its national soul like nothing since the Civil War. Dividing lines were bitterly drawn—not just between political parties and racial groups, but between generations and family members, sometimes even between siblings.

To fight or not to fight in Vietnam was the question. Some thought America should, some thought America shouldn't. Some youth eligible for military service went, some didn't. People were polarized in a way that still affects the country today. While marches, speeches, and protests raged, and news broadcasts reported body counts and beamed the latest images of combat into living rooms at dinnertime, hundreds of American soldiers were languishing as prisoners of war of the communist government of North Vietnam.

As the world later learned, their treatment by their captors constituted one of the most grievous violations of human rights in modern history. Some who were subsequently released reported being starved, beaten for hours on end, and chained and caged like animals for months. The longest-held captives faced the specter of such brutality for up to almost nine years. All the while, their loved ones back home wondered whether some of them were even still alive and whether they would ever see them again.

One veteran of the horror was Jeremiah Denton. A naval aviator, his plane was shot down over North Vietnam in July of 1965. For the next seven years and seven months, he suffered severe mistreatment, including four years in solitary confinement. In 1966, the North Vietnamese government arranged for him to appear in a televised interview to respond to allegations that they were committing atrocities. Ahead of the interview they threatened him with dire consequences if he failed to reply in a manner that protected their image. During the interview, however, Denton not only voiced support for the position of his government but, feigning sensitivity to the harsh television lights, blinked his eyes to spell out in Morse code: T-O-R-T-U-R-E.

For seven more years after that broadcast, Denton's family and the nation would pray and long for the release and return of Denton and his fellow captives. Multiple rounds of negotiations took place behind closed doors and on the international stage as well. Finally, in February 1973, Denton and others were released. As the ranking officer among the first group returning to Clark Air Force Base in the Philippines, Denton stepped from the plane upon landing and declared to the world: "We are honored to have had the opportunity to serve our country under difficult circumstances. We are profoundly grateful to our commander in chief and to our nation for this day. God bless America." Then followed a scene of ecstatic reunion between the newly freed survivors and their families, which was played out on television before a watching nation that also cheered and wept. News photos of the occasion have become classics, assuming their place as some of the most notable pictures ever taken. Many soldiers ran to embrace their loved ones, colliding with them full tilt and collapsing into their arms in a surreal moment of anticipation fulfilled. Others knelt and kissed the ground.

As President Ronald Reagan would recall in his 1982 State of the Union address—one for which Jeremiah Denton was seated in the audience: "We don't have to turn to our history books for heroes. They are all around us. One who sits among you here tonight epitomized that heroism at the end of the longest imprisonment ever inflicted on men of our armed forces. Who will ever forget that night when we waited for the television to bring us the scene of that first plane landing at Clark Field in the Philippines, bringing our POWs home. The plane door opened and Jeremiah Denton came slowly down the ramp. He caught sight of our flag, saluted, and said, 'God bless America,' then thanked us for bringing him home."

While longing for the return of American POWs dragged on for years (some are still missing and have never been accounted for), the anticipation of the coming of God's Son lasted for centuries. It must have seemed for those living before His appearance that He might never set foot on our earthly soil. One of the earliest recorded cries for Him came from a man named Job, who also suffered severely.

The Old Testament book that bears Job's name tells his story. Job lived in Uz, an ancient land most likely in the vicinity of the Dead Sea. Though upright, he lost his wealth, his health, and his children, causing his wife to urge him to curse God and die. In the midst of his grief and pain he maintained his faith but uttered a plea that has echoed through the centuries:

> Oh that I knew where I might find Him,
> that I might come to His seat! (Job 23:3).

God's plan, however, was to come to the hurting human race and take His seat here. His intention became increasingly apparent as He acted in the lives of those who, though they could not see Him, set their hearts on Him. Consider Abraham, for example.

After years of being childless, God gave Abraham and his wife Sarah their son Isaac when Abraham was 100 years old. Isaac embodied their hope for generations of descendants. Then, while Isaac was still a young boy, God called Abraham to offer him as a sacrifice—a literal sacrifice—a practice that was not uncommon in the pagan cultures of that day. The Bible records that Abraham proceeded to obey, even though as a father he must have been emotionally storm-tossed. "So Abraham rose early in the morning and saddled his donkey," the Scripture says, "and took...Isaac his son; and he split wood for the burnt offering, and arose and went to the place of which God had told him" (Genesis 22:3).

It must have been especially difficult for Abraham when Isaac, observing all of Abraham's preparations, said to him, "Behold, the fire and the wood, but where is the lamb for the burnt offering?" (verse 7). Abraham responded with a simple yet profound declaration of faith: "God will provide for Himself the lamb for the burnt offering, my son" (verse 8).

Later, Scripture gives us further insight into Abraham's faith in that moment: "He considered that God is able to raise people even from the dead" (Hebrews 11:19).

This confidence is what enabled Abraham to proceed with an act that, by all indications, would extinguish the life of his and Sarah's only begotten son. When they arrived, "Abraham built the altar there and arranged the wood, and bound his son Isaac and laid him on the altar, on top of the wood. Abraham stretched out his hand and took the knife to slay his son" (Genesis 22:9-10).

But the angle of the LORD called to him from heaven and said, "Abraham, Abraham!" And he said, "Here I am." He said, "Do not stretch out your hand against the lad, and do nothing to him; for now I know that you fear God, since you have not withheld your son, your only son, from Me." Then Abraham raised his eyes and looked, and behold, behind him a ram caught in the thicket by his horns; and Abraham went and took the ram and offered him up for a burnt offering in the place of his son (Genesis 22:9-13).

When we read this account today, it sounds bizarre. What kind of God, we ask, would call a man to sacrifice his son? Well, as God's response to Abraham's faith and obedience showed, God didn't want Abraham to kill his son—He wanted Abraham's heart, his highest affection, his greatest love. He wanted to see that He Himself meant more to Abraham than the blessings He had bestowed upon him. At the same time, He was foreshadowing the day that would dawn some 2000 years afterward on which His own Son—humanly speaking, a descendant of Abraham—would be killed as a sacrifice for the sins of the world. His Son would be the substitute who would die in our place. For Him there would be no last-second reprieve.

Some 400 years after Abraham, his descendant Moses—whom God used to lead the Israelites out of slavery in Egypt—saw even more of God's plan to come and take His seat among His people. As Moses and the Israelites sojourned in the wilderness en route to the land of Canaan, God revealed Himself to Moses on Mount Sinai. There He gave him the Ten Commandments, which are expressions of God's own character and the unrepealed moral law against which He measures every one of us today. He also prescribed to Moses the practices they were to observe as His chosen people living in the midst of idolatrous neighbors and spelled out to him His plan for the tabernacle—a tent they were to construct according to specific instructions, and in which God Himself would meet with them.

There, God would receive their offerings and sacrifices for their transgressions.

As human history and the history of Israel in particular continued to unfold, dealing with transgressions—the breaking of God's law—loomed as the central issue, for sin abounded not only among pagan people but among those to whom God had specially revealed Himself. Israel never completely drove out their idolatrous neighbors as God had commanded them, nor fully possessed the land. Despite the judges God gave His people to oversee their affairs and lead them in His way, they repeatedly rebelled and conducted themselves, in many instances, worse than those who did not worship God.

Later on, Israel expressed a desire for a human king—a desire God granted through Saul, who, by the end of his life, forsook God and resorted to consulting a medium for guidance. God next raised up David to succeed Saul and, while He declared David a man after His own heart (1 Samuel 13:14), David committed adultery and murder and brought trouble upon his house. After David's death, his son Solomon ascended to the throne.

During Solomon's reign, God authorized Solomon to construct a temple in Jerusalem as the place where He would dwell among His people. Even as it was completed in all of its grandeur, however, Solomon sensed the inadequacy of any building made with hands to contain the living God: "But will God indeed dwell with mankind on the earth? Behold, heaven and the highest heaven cannot contain You; how much less this house which I have built" (2 Chronicles 6:18).

Despite having such a visible reminder of God in their midst, God's people continued rebelling. After Solomon's death the kingdom of Israel divided into two and a string of kings—some better, some worse—reigned. Most of the tribes intermarried with foreigners and disappeared as a distinct race. Those who remained continued in sin to a point where God allowed the temple to be destroyed, Jerusalem sacked, and its inhabitants carried away into exile by the Babylonians. Even the voices of the prophets God sent to warn them, to call them back to Himself, to take them back to their land, and to give them fresh vision of a coming day of redemption eventually trailed off into silence.

For hundreds of years, in the life of the people who had once lived in the light of God's presence and experienced His grace and glory, it would seem to a great degree like hell was in session. Their experience would be like that of one prophet, who said, "I see him, but not now; I behold him, but not near" (Numbers 24:17).

The unfulfilled cry of their heart was, "Come, O come, Immanuel," which means "God with us" (Matthew 1:23). They were looking for God's anointed deliverer—Messiah, also called Christ. But it would be years before they could say, "Behold, this is our God for whom we have waited that He might save us. This is the LORD for whom we have waited; let us rejoice and be glad in His salvation" (Isaiah 25:9).

Still, the way for Him was being prepared.

Draw Near and Be Transformed

In His love for us God determined that, rather than being removed and aloof, He would take the initiative to come to where we are, in all of our questions, needs, and hurts. Have you allowed this wondrous truth to shape your view of Him and to be the starting point in your interaction with Him? How has it changed—or how might it change—the way you relate to Him?

5

Prepared

*Prepare the way of the LORD; make straight
in the desert a highway for our God.*

ISAIAH 40:3 NKJV

The stage was set; the world was waiting
for the arrival of God's Son.

When I was in college I was required—with the emphasis on *required*—to take a course that exposed me to the works of composers who were long dead but whose music, much to my puzzlement, had somehow managed not to fade into obscurity over time. You've got it—*classical* music.

Now please understand: As a teen who came of age surrounded by rock, any music that was more than ten years old, that didn't depend on electricity for its existence, and that didn't emit from speakers with a volume and force that could prove whether or not someone was wearing a toupee made me drowsy. Yet, there I was—my eyes were fixed on the goal of obtaining a college degree and, to do so, I had to attend a classical music concert. Woe was me!

Glenda and I were married by then and, like the supportive spouse she has always been, she agreed to go with me and babysit, er, enjoy the program with me. As we arrived in the concert hall we found our seats high in the balcony. I figured the whole experience might hurt less if we were sitting as far away as possible.

My first impressions were not positive. Dozens of musicians were seated in rows and wearing tuxedos—attire that I, as a jeans-clad college student, considered absurd. Before long I figured out that they were strategically arranged in sections—woodwinds, strings, brass, percussion, and so on. The sounds coming from them, however, were anything but orderly. In fact, the closest parallel I could think of was the chaotic noise of a carnival, where you hear drifting through the air a flood of sound bites that don't connect to one another.

Soon, however, things changed. A man I came to realize was the conductor strode confidently onto the stage and stood facing the musicians. They grew silent and focused on him intently. Then, he raised into the air a baton that, from our seats, looked like a toothpick. And, with a sweep of his arms, he summoned forth a powerful convergence of harmonic tones. It was as if he had said, "Let there be music!"

As melodic strains filled the hall, something happened. I was watching and listening and beginning to think that maybe I'd be able to survive this experience without too much pain when I felt something warm on my face, just above my mouth. No, it wasn't a tear of joy. Touching it, then looking at my fingers in the dimly lit hall, I saw that my nose had begun to bleed. Whether it was caused by this strange music or just the elevation of our seats, I wasn't sure. All I knew was that I now had a medical reason to excuse myself from the concert and I was out of there!

Since then I've learned to appreciate, at least in some measure, the subtleties and nuances of such music. In fact, I've realized that much of what we now refer to as classical music was actually created for worship and was, when written, the "contemporary Christian music" of its day. I'm not proud of it, but I have to admit that sometimes I even tune into classical music while driving in my car. Lest I become too cultured, however, I change it before long to a country music station!

There's a picture here worth noting: The Lord God Almighty, since before He spoke creation into being, has been orchestrating all things to harmoniously converge and culminate in the glory, honor, and worship of His Son, the Lord Jesus Christ. That's why history *is* His story.

In the time now viewed as the hinge of history—that period of transition from B.C. (before Christ) to A.D. (*anno Domini*, Latin for "in the year of our Lord") and that others refer to as the shift from B.C.E. (before the common era) to C.E. (the common era)—human affairs were indeed converging in ways that would facilitate the appearance of God's Son, the fulfillment of His mission, and the rapid imprint of His gospel upon the world.

The Roman Empire was in full bloom and enjoying a sustained period of relative tranquility. Its military and legal systems provided a measure of stability over the portion of the globe Rome ruled. A vast system of roads made travel easier, while shared currencies and dialects promoted trade. Religious practices of every description— austere, extravagant, reverent, lewd—were rife. For their part, the Jews who were dispersed across the empire had established a system of synagogues, or places for meeting, instruction, and discussion, that were key centers of interaction and influence.

The stage was set and the world was waiting for the arrival of God's Son. Finally, into the mundane humdrum of everyday existence would come a voice, a voice that would thunder from the void of the Judean wilderness, a voice that would stir the people and shake the Jewish establishment, a voice of knowing urgency. Through Malachi the prophet, God Himself told of this voice in advance: "Behold, I am going to send My messenger, and he will clear the way before Me. And the Lord, whom you seek, will suddenly come…and the messenger of the covenant, in whom you delight, behold, He is coming" (Malachi 3:1).

This heaven-sent messenger would cut across the grain of anything politically correct—either in dress or diet or social sensibilities. Yet the One he was sent to herald would eventually say that "among those born of women there has not arisen anyone greater" (Matthew 11:11).

One writer would sum up this messenger's mission in these words: "There came a man sent from God.... He came as a witness, to testify about the Light, so that all might believe through him. He was not the Light, but he came to testify about the Light" (John 1:6-8).

The message that would reverberate from the depths of the messenger's rugged frame could be summarized in the words of Isaiah: " 'Prepare the way of the LORD; make straight in the desert a highway for our God' " (Isaiah 40:3 NKJV).

The messenger was John the Baptist, son of an aged Jewish priest named Zacharias and his previously barren wife, Elizabeth. As John was born and, later, as he carried on his unorthodox ministry, a buzz swept through the multitudes. They wondered what strange thing was coming to pass.

The answer was that the divine orchestra that had been tuning up since creation, and even before, was now about to sound its opening chord. What a chord it would be!

Draw Near and Be Transformed

Perhaps you've wanted for a long time to know God personally but still wonder whether you can. Let me ask: Can you allow for the possibility that God Himself has been working through the experiences and circumstances of your life to bring you to this very moment, a moment when He wants to reveal Himself to you in the person of His Son, the Lord Jesus Christ, in a way that will transform you forever?

God is even more eager to be known by you than you are to know Him. Rejoice and read on—your time has come!

Part Two:

While He Was Here

When the fullness of the time came,
God sent forth His Son...

GALATIANS 4:4

6

*Therefore the Lord Himself will give you a sign:
Behold, a virgin will be with child and bear a
son, and she will call His name Immanuel.*

ISAIAH 7:14

God has the ability to do anything that
is consistent with His nature.

Famed talk show host Larry King is perhaps the best-known broadcast personality in the world. A journalism professional for a half-century, he has interviewed thousands of people on his live call-in program televised across the globe on CNN. His guests have ranged from heads of state to movie stars to athletes to criminals. When asked, however, which individual he would most want to interview if he could choose anyone from all of history, he is quoted as answering, "Jesus Christ."

Why?

Because, King said, "I would like to ask Him if He was indeed virgin-born. The answer to that question would define history for me."

Larry King was right. The uniqueness of Christ's conception is not some incidental subject for casual speculation. Both His nature and His mission depend upon it.

The only way Jesus could be God's Son while at the same time being a real human being was for God Himself to bring about His conception in the womb of a woman. And because all of us inherit from our parents a bent toward sin and then choose it for ourselves and practice it wholeheartedly, the only way Christ could be adequate to deal with human sin was for Him to maintain His sinless divine nature even while entering and being part of a fallen human race. That's likely why the virgin birth of Jesus Christ has been one of the most hotly debated subjects of our time.

Having said that, I need to admit something, though I do so at the risk of being misunderstood: *I'm somewhat amused that people stumble over the idea that the Son of God could be born to a virgin.*

Let me hurriedly go on to say that I mean no disrespect for anyone to whom this truth is a serious point of struggle. It's just that, in my mind, the question of *how* God would enter into the human race pales in view of the wonder that He would do so at all!

God, after all, has the ability to do anything that is consistent with His nature…so causing a virgin—a woman who had never engaged in sexual relations—to bear a child isn't inconceivable (pardon the pun). To be sure it is miraculous—that is, it's an occasion when the natural state of things is superseded by a greater will and force—and it has profound implications. The natural state of things is superseded by greater will and force daily, however, even in ways that we don't consider miraculous.

At a gym near our house, for example, men and women lift above their heads masses of steel weighing more than they do and that would otherwise just rest motionless on the floor, and they do it multiple times, focusing their personal will and force on superseding another force known as gravity (notice I said *they* do it, not *I!*). Granted, they accomplish this feat only temporarily, but at least for a time they prevail. Why is it so difficult to believe that God can interpose and assert Himself into situations any time He chooses?

In our day even human reproduction is being accomplished by other than traditional means. Without being too explicit about the anatomy of it all, women who have never engaged in sexual intercourse are giving birth through in vitro fertilization and embryonic transfer. Some are even putting their eggs into freezers for later use… a practice considered preposterous not too many years ago!

So, is it really all that unthinkable that God, the Author of life and all its processes, would move upon a chaste young woman so that she would conceive and give birth to a Son, and that He would do so in a way that overshadowed and superseded the usual process? Not for me—nor, according to polls, for roughly eight out of ten Americans!

Notwithstanding the foolishness of many modern clergy who express their disbelief in the virgin birth at a rate far higher than even the general population, Christians throughout the centuries have recognized and affirmed the literal fulfillment of the angel's announcement to a young Jewish virgin called Mary: "Do not be afraid, Mary; for you have found favor with God. And behold, you will conceive in your womb and bear a son, and you shall name Him Jesus. He will be great and will be called the Son of the Most High" (Luke 1:30-32).

The Apostles' Creed, in use by the middle of the second century as a foundational declaration of the core truths of the Christian faith, says:

> I believe in God, the Father Almighty,
> the Creator of heaven and earth,
> and in Jesus Christ, His only Son, our Lord:
>
> Who was conceived of the Holy Spirit,
> born of the Virgin Mary…

Numerous later creeds declared the same conviction, usually to counter and correct some wind of heresy blowing through that particular day. In the sixteenth century, for example, the great reformer Martin Luther elaborated on the Apostles' Creed by writing, "I believe that Jesus Christ, true God, begotten of the Father from eternity, and also true man, born of the Virgin Mary, is my Lord."

It's important to note that Martin Luther moved from entertaining a concept to embracing a person, the Person of God's Son, the Lord Jesus Christ. That's what God desires and delights for each of us to do. It's also what Mary had to do when she received the angel's announcement:

> Mary said to the angel, "How can this be, since I am a virgin?" The angel answered and said to her, "The Holy Spirit will come upon you, and the power of the Most High will overshadow you; and for that reason the holy Child shall be called the Son of God.... For nothing will be impossible with God" (Luke 1:34-35,37).

At that point Mary went from considering to clinging. A fallen sinner just like the rest of us, she nonetheless yielded herself to God for Him to do with, in, and through her whatever He pleased: "And Mary said, 'Behold, the bondslave of the Lord; may it be done to me according to your word'" (verse 38).

Joseph, the man who became Mary's husband, also had to come to terms with the manner of Christ's conception, for it certainly impacted him. Scripture records that, before Mary and Joseph

> came together she was found to be with child by the Holy Spirit. And Joseph her husband, being a righteous man and not wanting to disgrace her, planned to send her away secretly. But when he had considered this, behold, an angel of the Lord appeared to him in a dream, saying, "Joseph, son of David, do not be afraid to take Mary as your wife; for the Child who has been conceived in her is of the Holy Spirit. She will bear a Son; and you shall call His name Jesus, for He will save His people from their sins" (Matthew 1:18-21).

When Joseph "awoke from his sleep," he "did as the angel of the Lord commanded him, and took Mary as his wife, but kept her a virgin until she gave birth to a Son; and he called His name Jesus" (verses 24-25).

For those of us living in a society that promotes selfishness, instant gratification, and irresponsibility through cohabitation and sex outside marriage, Joseph was a shining example of selflessness and obedience to God. He took to himself a wife he knew was carrying a child who was God's and not his own. In doing so he also took upon himself the misunderstanding, gossip, and ridicule that her pregnancy would provoke. And even after he and Mary became husband and wife, he delayed enjoying physical intimacy with his beautiful young bride for months, till after she had given birth. Now that, my friend, is a *real* man, which is likely why God chose to entrust His only begotten Son to his care!

Let's go back to the *how* question. *How* did God bring to pass in Mary's womb this wondrous event? By the Holy Spirit.

The Bible presents the one true living God as Father, as Son, and as Spirit—three Persons who are distinct yet at the same time co-existent and equal, each with His own unique role. How this can be transcends the limits of our finite minds, but from God's perspective, that's the way it is. The Holy Spirit is not just some nebulous, ethereal force. Consistently in Scripture, the Holy Spirit is referred to as a "He" and not an "It." Though unseen, He has great power—indeed, all the power of God.

The power of the Holy Spirit was operative in creation. During the ensuing centuries, the power of the Holy Spirit bore upon human affairs again and again to accomplish the purposes of God. The power of the Holy Spirit caused Mary to conceive. The power of the Holy Spirit would be continuously evident in the life and ministry of the Child she would bear. Today, among other aspects of His work, the power of the Holy Spirit is moving in people's hearts and lives—including yours and mine—to draw us into an ever-deepening relationship with God.

As Mary and Joseph were about to discover, the birth of Jesus would also become quite a draw!

DRAW NEAR AND BE TRANSFORMED

Do you sense the Holy Spirit working in your heart to draw you into a deeper relationship with God? In what ways?

Are you willing with Mary—who yielded herself to God for Him to do with, in, and through her whatever He pleased—to move from merely considering information *about* Christ to clinging *to* Christ? If not, what's holding you back?

Are you prepared to move from entertaining a concept to embracing a person, the Person of Christ, in all of His wonder? Why wait?

Take a moment right now to say to Him, "I believe that You, Jesus Christ, are truly God, that You were begotten of the Father from eternity, and that You are also truly man, being born of the virgin Mary, and I wholeheartedly embrace You as my Lord. Thank You for loving me."

7

Born

*Today in the city of David there has been
born for you a Savior, who is Christ the Lord.*

LUKE 2:11

Right there before the shepherds in that small,
fragile body was the One whose coming had
been foretold and anticipated for centuries.

For a combination of excitement and terror, nothing quite matches the birth of one's first child. (I'm speaking, of course, from a father's perspective—Glenda is quick to point out to me that I know absolutely nothing about what a woman goes through in childbirth!)

The births of all four of our children were memorably unique. I was speaking in a church in another state when Glenda went into labor with our youngest, JesseRuth. Labor lasted long enough for me to drive several hundred miles in order to be present. (We won't talk about speed limits!) For Nathan's arrival, we were at the hospital only about 45 minutes before he arrived on the scene. Gregory took about 12 hours to appear. Hannah took just about that long as well…but something about the birth of that first child can cause the steeliest of men to melt in the face of the wonder and the weighty responsibility of it all.

I'll never forget seeing this just-delivered baby girl take her first breath, open her eyes wide, then stick out her tongue at the obstetrician. That was our first clue into both the delights and challenges that awaited us as her parents. I remember wondering whether I would be up to the task. I'm thankful to say that God has been faithful, Glenda and I have survived, and today Hannah is a godly woman and wife.

I wonder how Joseph felt as the birth of Jesus approached. There he was, a simple carpenter whose skill was in making things with wood, yet the baby growing in Mary's womb was "the image of the invisible God, the firstborn of all creation.... by Him all things were created, both in the heavens and on earth, visible and invisible, whether thrones or dominions or rulers or authorities" (Colossians 1:15-16).

When holding the infant in his arms, Joseph would be holding the One in whom "all the fullness of Deity dwells in bodily form" (Colossians 2:9). New fathers are usually clumsy at best with their babies—this truth would certainly raise the stakes!

Then, too, there were the extraordinary circumstances and events surrounding Jesus' birth, not the least of which was the visitation by multiple angels, not only to Mary but also to others. In his Gospel account, Luke—a physician by profession—wrote this timeless narrative:

> Now in those days a decree went out from Caesar Augustus, that a census be taken of all the inhabited earth. This was the first census taken while Quirinius was governor of Syria. And everyone was on his way to register for the census, each to his own city. Joseph also went up from Galilee, from the city of Nazareth, to Judea, to the city of David which is called Bethlehem, because he was of the house and family of David, in order to register along with Mary, who was engaged to

him, and was with child. While they were there, the days were completed for her to give birth. And she gave birth to her firstborn son; and she wrapped Him in cloths, and laid Him in a manger, because there was no room for them in the inn.

In the same region there were some shepherds staying out in the fields and keeping watch over their flock by night. And an angel of the Lord suddenly stood before them, and the glory of the Lord shone around them; and they were terribly frightened. But the angel said to them, "Do not be afraid; for behold, I bring you good news of great joy which will be for all the people; for today in the city of David there has been born for you a Savior, who is Christ the Lord. This will be a sign for you: you will find a baby wrapped in cloths and lying in a manger." And suddenly there appeared with the angel a multitude of the heavenly host praising God and saying, "Glory to God in the highest, And on earth peace among men with whom He is pleased."

When the angels had gone away from them into heaven, the shepherds began saying to one another, "Let us go straight to Bethlehem then, and see this thing that has happened which the Lord has made known to us." So they came in a hurry and found their way to Mary and Joseph, and the baby as He lay in the manger. When they had seen this, they made known the statement which had been told them about this Child. And all who heard it wondered at the things which were told them by the shepherds. But Mary treasured all these things, pondering them in her heart. The shepherds went back, glorifying and praising God for all that they had heard and seen, just as had been told them (Luke 2:1-20).

I'm not aware that I've ever actually seen with my physical eyes an angel from heaven operating here in the earthly realm, though on several occasions when I've been in danger or special need I have sensed their presence. Scripture urges us not to "neglect to show hospitality to strangers, for by this some have entertained angels without knowing it" (Hebrews 13:2).

When Christ was born, however, there was no mistaking it—shepherds used to watching over a bunch of bleating sheep suddenly saw and heard heavenly beings announcing this unprecedented event and proclaiming God's praises. The shepherds hurried to see this sight for themselves and found things exactly as the angels declared—a baby, wrapped in strips of cloth similar to those used for burial, lying in, of all places, a feeding trough for animals!

As Mary and Joseph received these visitors and allowed them to gaze upon the baby in the strange surroundings of their make-shift nursery, on display for the first time was the One whom God had "appointed heir of all things, through whom also He made the world," the One who "is the radiance of His glory and the exact representation of His nature, and upholds all things by the word of His power" (Hebrews 1:2-3).

Right there before the shepherds in that small, fragile body was the One who had existed before the beginning, the One whose coming had been foretold and anticipated for centuries, the One who would put an end to Satan's deception and destruction, the One who would save people from their sins, the One who would come to reign over everything.

The shepherds responded to all this with rejoicing. But it wouldn't be very long before others responded to the news of Christ's birth far differently.

DRAW NEAR AND BE TRANSFORMED

How do you respond to the news that a Savior was born for you?

Have you, like the shepherds, personally inquired and come to know Him for yourself? Or is your knowledge of Him still second-hand, something announced to you by your parents, a friend, or someone else, but that you yourself haven't yet experienced?

What's to keep you from doing so right now?

8

Threatened

Get up…take the child and his mother and escape to Egypt. Stay there until I tell you, for Herod is going to search for the child to kill him.

MATTHEW 2:13 NIV

The serpent of old had Christ in his crosshairs and was determined to do what he could to undermine the mission for which He came to earth.

It was the day after Christmas.

Small children played while villagers went about their usual chores—cooking, washing, farming, fishing. Merchants in the market were displaying their wares in hopes of getting a good price for them. Adults were discussing, even arguing about, politics and religion. The blazing sun filling the clear sky brought perspiration to the brow. The cool water that perpetually lapped at the shore beckoned.

On this day, however, something was amiss. At first just a few people noticed it. Word spread quickly, however, and soon it was on everyone's lips. Did it mean what they thought? Could it really be happening? What should they do?

Elders hurriedly conferred and made their decision. They had to take the signs seriously. After all, they knew their history and remembered what had happened to those who had previously ignored them. Hoping for the best but fearing the worst, they issued their order: Head for high ground.

Within minutes, a giant wall of water surged across the village, leveling everything in its path. The Asian tsunami of December 26, 2004 had struck. One of the deadliest disasters in history, it killed hundreds of thousands of people and caused massive damage across thousands of miles.

On the island of Simuelue, however, the death toll was reportedly not nearly as severe as elsewhere. Incredibly, only seven of 78,000 inhabitants died, even though the tsunami hit there just eight minutes after an earthquake in the Indian Ocean west of Sumatra, Indonesia, spawned it.

Why? Because a century earlier, another earthquake-induced tsunami had hit the village and survivors of that event had passed down word of the warning signs—a series of larger-than-normal waves, for example, accompanied by unusual quantities of marine life on the beach and a marked recession of the sea.

These villagers recognized the signs and fled for their lives while they still could. Their vigilance and responsiveness paid off. People living in other areas that had even more time to respond but did not, however, suffered horrific casualties, with populations of entire towns being obliterated.

After Jesus was born in Bethlehem "during the time of King Herod" (Matthew 2:1 NIV), Joseph and Mary found themselves faced with a similarly urgent warning. Scripture tells the story:

> Magi [wise men] from the east came to Jerusalem and asked, "Where is the one who has been born king of the Jews? We saw his star in the east and have come to worship him."
>
> When King Herod heard this he was disturbed, and all

Jerusalem with him. When he had called together all the people's chief priests and teachers of the law, he asked them where the Christ was to be born. "In Bethlehem in Judea," they replied, "for this is what the prophet has written: 'But you, Bethlehem, in the land of Judah, are by no means least among the rulers of Judah; for out of you will come a ruler who will be the shepherd of my people Israel.'"[6]

Then Herod called the Magi secretly and found out from them the exact time the star had appeared. He sent them to Bethlehem and said, "Go and make a careful search for the child. As soon as you find him, report to me, so that I too may go and worship him."

After they had heard the king, they went on their way, and the star they had seen in the east went ahead of them until it stopped over the place where the child was. When they saw the star, they were overjoyed. On coming to the house, they saw the child with his mother Mary, and they bowed down and worshiped him. Then they opened their treasures and presented him with gifts of gold and of incense and of myrrh. And having been warned in a dream not to go back to Herod, they returned to their country by another route (verses 1-12 NIV).

Next came a warning to Joseph:

When they had gone, an angel of the Lord appeared to Joseph in a dream. "Get up," he said, "take the child and his mother and escape to Egypt. Stay there until I tell you, for Herod is going to search for the child to kill him." So he got up, took the child and his mother during the night and left for Egypt, where he stayed until the death of Herod (Matthew 2:13-15 NIV).

Herod, however, was not about to let the matter rest.

When Herod realized that he had been outwitted by the Magi, he was furious, and he gave orders to kill all the boys in Bethlehem and its vicinity who were two years old and under, in accordance with the time he had learned from the Magi. Then what was said through the prophet Jeremiah was fulfilled: "A voice is heard in Ramah, weeping and great mourning, Rachel weeping for her children and refusing to be comforted, because they are no more" (verses 16-18 NIV).

While this incident—which came to be known as the Slaughter of the Innocents—rightly repulses us, it was completely in keeping with Herod's character. During his 36-year reign he committed multiple atrocities, even within his own family. The common understanding was that it was "better to be Herod's dog than one of his children."

Yet Herod's murderous scheme against the male babies in Bethlehem was not just some random act of violence. It was a deliberate, systematic attempt from hell to kill the Lord Jesus. Even at this early point in His life, "the serpent of old who is called the devil and Satan" (Revelation 12:9) had Christ in his crosshairs and was determined to do what he could to oppose and undermine the mission for which He came to earth.

Why? Because "the Son of God appeared for this purpose, to destroy the works of the devil" (1 John 3:8). The wickedness in Herod's heart gave Satan a beachhead from which he could wage an assault on the Son of God. The devout man to whom God had entrusted Him, however, heeded the heavenly warnings, took the prescribed action, and Christ was spared for the work that lay ahead of Him.

At this point you may find yourself saying, "that's all well and good…but what about those other children? Doesn't it matter that they died in the process?" Of course it does. Sin, however, inevitably hurts many people, not just those directly responsible for it. This incident demonstrates, at least in some measure, sin's awful ugliness and underscores why we should avoid it at all cost. Whenever we pursue a path contrary to Christ, others, too, will suffer.

Even as we're justifiably indignant about what happened to those children of old, it's important to recognize that innocent children are still dying today as a result of choices by their elders. Children are usually the ones who suffer most from wars they did not start, from poverty they did not cause, from their parents' addictions to alcohol and drugs, and from diseases such as AIDS to which they did not expose themselves. And daily they are the victims of choices made by people who act in a manner that leads to the conception of human life but who are not subsequently willing to accept the responsibility for the person they bring into being, electing instead to terminate—to murder—him or her prior to birth.

Joseph and Mary, however, were not willing to sacrifice their child on the altar of convenience. Rather, they embraced God's surprise gift to them and took responsibility for His well-being. To protect Him they uprooted themselves yet again and made the arduous journey to Egypt and stayed there, some 350 miles from their family and familiar surroundings, until danger was past. Then:

> After Herod died, an angel of the Lord appeared in a dream to Joseph in Egypt and said, "Get up, take the child and his mother and go to the land of Israel, for those who were trying to take the child's life are dead." So he got up, took the child and his mother and went to the land of Israel. But when he heard that Archelaus was reigning in Judea in place of his father Herod, he was afraid to go there. Having been warned in a dream, he withdrew to the district of Galilee, and he went and lived in a town called Nazareth. So was fulfilled what was said through the prophets: "He will be called a Nazarene" (Matthew 2:19-23 NIV).

There in Nazareth, Jesus would grow in ways that would startle even those closest to Him.

DRAW NEAR AND BE TRANSFORMED

Have you ever sensed that God, in His love for you, was giving you a warning sign that you needed to heed? How did you respond? What was the outcome?

Even the fact that you are reading these words urging you to trust Christ for forgiveness and salvation may be a gracious warning from God for your own well-being. Have you done so?

If you're already a follower of Christ, in what way might God be speaking to you right now to keep you from a course of action that could be damaging, even devastating for you and others? Will you heed His warning and "head for high ground"?

9

Growing

*The Child continued to grow and become
strong, increasing in wisdom;
and the grace of God was upon Him.*

LUKE 2:40

As Jesus approached the traditional age of
adulthood for Jewish males, the reason for His
coming to earth was foremost in His mind.

What are your family's traditions?

Most families have some and return to them over and over as cherished markers of their lives together through the years. Each successive one becomes a point of reference for family members' ages and activities during a particular season of life, whether as a preschooler, student, working adult, or retiree. Holidays such as Christmas and Easter are prime times for family traditions, but other occasions work as well, and the traditions observed are as unique as each family. A friend told me recently, for example, that his south Georgia family has gathered to cook Christmas barbecue in the same pit on the same farm for generations. In another family I know, every Mother's Day is when all the men go fishing—go figure!

Somehow, I don't think we'd ever be able to pull that off in our family, but we do have some traditions of our own, due largely to Glenda's loving initiative. One is that every Christmas Eve, she gives everybody a new pair of pajamas, which we all wear as we gather around the tree the next morning. The result is that, in our early Christmas morning photos, we all look like we just stepped out of a catalog (not!).

Another tradition in our family is that Glenda's birthday holds the same status as a national holiday and no amount of pageantry is considered excessive. In fact, I live and die the rest of the year by how well I orchestrate her birthday celebration. I'm still trying to live down a few of my underwhelming performances!

Jesus' family had traditions as well. Scripture tells us that, in the small town of Nazareth, He "continued to grow and become strong, increasing in wisdom; and the grace of God was upon Him" (Luke 2:40). One factor in His growth in wisdom and grace was His family's tradition of traveling to Jerusalem each year to celebrate the Jewish feast of Passover.

At some point, this annual trip must have become quite an effort. Scripture tells us that Joseph and Mary together eventually had at least six children (four sons, two daughters) and Jesus, which made for quite a brood! The usual route between Nazareth and Jerusalem was about 240 miles round trip. For Passover, extended families and entire villages thronged to Jerusalem, merging into caravans of walkers that extended as far as the eye could see. Typically the travelers would camp along the way. Imagining what this journey must have been like for two parents with a bunch of energetic kids, I think of that time-honored tradition known as a *family vacation,* which our family and most others have experienced. Oh, the joys of it!

> *I can't wait to go on vacation.*
> *I have so much to do to get ready.*
> *Tommy, I just packed that...why are you taking it out of the suitcase?*

Yes, Tommy, you do need more than one pair of underwear for two weeks.

No, you can't take the goldfish.

Stand back—I'm loading the car!

No, you can't ride in the trunk.

We can't put more than eight bikes on the back of the car.

Why am I sweating? Because packing is hard work.

I didn't yell at you.

Okay! We're all loaded...let's go.

Tommy, you sit in the middle.

Are we there yet?

Tommy has to go to the bathroom.

Tommy just threw up on me.

Mommy, why are you crying?

Are we there yet?

Gee, this is fun.

My ice cream's melting.

Tommy hit me.

Tommy, tell your sister you're sorry.

You know, they really are great kids.

I hate to have to go back home.

Are we there yet?

It's good to be home.

I can't wait till next year.

Where's Tommy???

Jesus was a perfect son and brother—in fact, the only one there's ever been, despite what many doting parents think. And He certainly wasn't the family troublemaker. Even so, His years of growing to maturity, on which the Bible is largely silent, held at least one surprise.

It occurred "when He became twelve," and His family went up

to Jerusalem "according to the custom of the Feast" (Luke 2:42). Afterward, when everyone began returning home, "the boy Jesus stayed behind in Jerusalem. But His parents were unaware of it, but supposed Him to be in the caravan, and went a day's journey; and they began looking for Him among their relatives and acquaintances" (Luke 2:43-44).

Every parent who, in a crowd, has suddenly realized that their child is not where they thought and that, in fact, they have no idea where he or she is knows that gut-tightening impulse of panic that comes over you at such an instant. It happened to Glenda and me when Nathan was two or three and wandered off in a shopping mall while we were looking at some merchandise. While trying to keep up with Gregory and Hannah, who were just a little older, we hurriedly searched the store—to no avail—then alerted mall security. All the while our minds were racing. No matter how much we wanted to push it down, the question kept popping to the surface: Had Nathan been abducted? Thankfully, in a little-while-that-seemed-like-forever a guard appeared with our toddler in tow. He had found Nathan happily munching away at a candy kiosk. Jesus' parents did not find their son as quickly.

> When they did not find Him, they returned to Jerusalem looking for Him. Then, after three days they found Him in the temple, sitting in the midst of the teachers, both listening to them and asking them questions. And all who heard Him were amazed at His understanding and His answers. When they saw Him, they were astonished; and His mother said to Him, "Son, why have You treated us this way? Behold, Your father and I have been anxiously looking for You." And He said to them, "Why is it that you were looking for Me? Did you not know that I had to be in My Father's house?" But they did not understand the statement which He had made to them (Luke 2:45-50).

In acting and responding as He did, Jesus was not being inconsiderate or rude to His parents. Rather, as He approached the traditional age of adulthood for Jewish males, the reason for His coming to earth was foremost in His mind. For the One who was the Word made flesh, it was absolutely consistent for Him to be discussing the Scriptures with the Jewish leaders in the temple. The point of Christ's question to Mary and Joseph was why they didn't look for Him there sooner rather than later, immediately rather than after several days.

As a friend of mine says, "they lost Him because they were depending on past experience...they lost Him because they were depending on others to keep up with Him...and they found Him exactly where they left Him" (insights that can apply to many people today!).[7]

Jesus was also asserting to His parents that His relationship to His heavenly Father took precedence over even His most cherished earthly relationships—a perspective He would later declare as a condition of discipleship. "For whoever does the will of My Father who is in heaven," He said, "he is My brother and sister and mother" (Matthew 12:50).

This was likely a moment of learning for Mary and Joseph—something that often occurs in the course of parenting. Nonetheless, Jesus "went down with them and came to Nazareth, and He continued in subjection to them; and His mother treasured all these things in her heart. And Jesus kept increasing in wisdom and stature, and in favor with God and men" (Luke 2:51-52).

Even though Jesus was the King of kings and Lord of lords, His attitude of submission was consistently evident all through His life and ministry.

DRAW NEAR AND BE TRANSFORMED

What traditions in your life have given you greater glimpses of God's character and ways and helped you draw nearer to Him?

How are you attempting to help those closest to you to grow in their experience of God's wisdom and favor?

If you have children, what moments of personal learning have you yourself experienced while parenting them?

Does your relationship with God take precedence over even your most cherished human relationships—with your employer, your coworkers, your friends, your parents, your children, your spouse? If not, why not?

10

Submitting

Then Jesus arrived from Galilee at the Jordan coming to John, to be baptized by him.

MATTHEW 3:13

Jesus' lifelong attitude of submission to His Father's will was operative even in this seemingly small matter.

I really like a good pair of cowboy boots.

My penchant for them began when I was a young boy. They made me feel like I could ride a horse, wrangle a steer, and hunt down a train robber in the Wild West. I remember having a pair that I outgrew before very long. Not the easiest footwear to get onto a squirming kid's feet, I don't think my mother was too eager to replace them. Still, though, I had developed a preference for them. As soon as I became old enough to pick out my own shoes I began choosing boots, even though they weren't especially popular among my friends.

Today I've come to admire the craftsmanship that goes into a handmade pair of boots. Designing them for their intended function as well as for orthopedic comfort, selecting appropriate leathers and skins, sewing intricate stitching, tooling custom designs—

mastering this process requires skill, careful attention to detail, and usually a period of apprenticeship.

I wear boots for most occasions—work, church, weddings, funerals, traveling, jogging (Just kidding about that last one!). Glenda says I wear them with suits as a silent protest that, while I'm all dressed up, I really don't want to be. Actually, they feel sturdier to me than other shoes, and I like having the protection around my ankles and calves...after all, you never know when a snake might try to bite you! They also remind me of some words from the late Corrie ten Boom, who, with her family, suffered greatly for hiding Jews from the Nazis in Holland during World War II:

"If God sends us on strong paths," she said, "we are provided strong shoes."

In the rough-and-tumble of life, we've personally experienced this truth...but more on that later.

Boot making began in ancient Mesopotamia thousands of years before Christ appeared. In the first-century Roman Empire, boots were worn especially by soldiers, who put hobnails on the soles, and by members of the upper class, such as government officials. Eventually others wore them too, but most commoners wore sandals or walked barefooted. The archaeological digs at Qumran—where the famed Dead Sea scrolls were found—have yielded sandals from the period that were essentially layers of hide with strips of leather used to attach them to the feet.

According to Scripture, Jesus apparently wore sandals. This detail emerges during the ministry of John the Baptist, who, with his shaggy locks, his garment of camel's hair and leather belt, and his diet of locusts and wild honey must have seemed like something of a first-century cowboy to the hordes of people who flocked to hear his message in the Judean wilderness. "Repent," he told them bluntly, "for the kingdom of heaven is at hand....make ready the way of the Lord, make His paths straight!" (Matthew 3:2-3).

When John the Baptist's listeners confessed and turned from their sins, he baptized them, dipping them in the waters of the

Jordan River. This was a symbol of the cleansing and renewal God offers those who come to Him in contrition and faith. At the same time, however, John plainly told his hearers that he was but a shadow of the One to come who would administer not just an external ritual but who would transform hearts and permanently deal with evil.

> As for me, I baptize you with water for repentance, but He who is coming after me is mightier than I, and I am not fit to remove His sandals; He will baptize you with the Holy Spirit and fire. His winnowing fork is in His hand, and He will thoroughly clear His threshing floor; and He will gather His wheat into the barn, but He will burn up the chaff with unquenchable fire (Matthew 3:11-12).

Notice John's words, "I am not fit to remove His sandals." The custom of the day was that, when a guest entered a home, the household slave would untie the visitor's sandals, wash the dust off his feet, and perhaps even remove the soil from his sandals by slapping them against an outside wall. This was a lowly chore that, while showing hospitality and conferring dignity on the guest, underscored the servant's position of abasement.

In speaking of the coming One, John declared that he wasn't worthy to assume even that humble role in relation to Him. Indeed, when he saw Jesus approaching he told his followers, "Behold, the Lamb of God who takes away the sin of the world! This is He on behalf of whom I said, 'After me comes a Man who has a higher rank than I, for He existed before me'" (John 1:29-30).

What a contrast to the presumption and arrogance of many people today who speak flippantly, even blasphemously, about Christ! Even more striking, however, is the way Christ responded to John.

> Then Jesus arrived from Galilee at the Jordan coming to John, to be baptized by him. But John tried to prevent Him, saying, "I have need to be baptized by You, and do You come to me?" But Jesus answering said to him,

"Permit it at this time; for in this way it is fitting for
us to fulfill all righteousness." Then he permitted Him
(Matthew 3:13-15).

Jesus didn't argue to John that He Himself wasn't worthy of the
position of exaltation that John was ascribing to Him. Rather, He
affirmed John's work of preparing the way for Him by submitting
to John's baptism, even though He was sinless.

A nice gesture?

Yes…but Jesus' submission on this occasion was far more than
that. He Himself would later declare that "he who is faithful in a
very little thing is faithful also in much; and he who is unrighteous
in a very little thing is unrighteous also in much" (Luke 16:10). His
lifelong attitude of submission to His Father's will, which would
ultimately result in His horrifying death on the cross, was operative
even in this seemingly small matter. The significance of Jesus' act
was not lost on John, nor was it lost on His heavenly Father.

After being baptized, Jesus came up immediately from
the water; and behold, the heavens were opened, and he
saw the Spirit of God descending as a dove and lighting
on Him, and behold, a voice out of the heavens said,
"This is My beloved Son, in whom I am well-pleased"
(Matthew 3:16-17).

Following this event, God's beloved Son looked past the crowd
beside the Jordan and walked on down the road to take care of the
business His Father had assigned to Him. His next appointment
was in the wilderness.

DRAW NEAR AND BE TRANSFORMED

Can you recall a time when you "repented"—that is, expressed to God your sorrow for your sins and committed yourself to turning away from them? What happened?

Did your repentance result in a new way of living? Why or why not?

Many people seem to have the attitude that they are in a position to negotiate with God and try to bargain with Him. Others, such as John the Baptist, view themselves as being unworthy to perform even the lowliest of tasks for Christ and instead declare their need to be transformed by Him. Which way do you approach Jesus?

Does the idea that Christ will permanently deal with evil cause you fear or give you hope? Why?

Christ's lifelong attitude of submission to His Father's will was reflected even in seemingly small matters. How committed are you to pleasing God by obeying Him in the details of your relationships and activities?

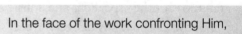

11

Praying

*Jesus Himself would often slip
away to the wilderness and pray.*

LUKE 5:16

In the face of the work confronting Him,
Christ made prayer His ongoing priority.

The National Prayer Breakfast, held annually in Washington, D.C., for over 50 years now, is like no other occasion.

This meal on the first Thursday morning of each February is the capstone for several days of seminars—conducted "in the name and spirit of Jesus of Nazareth," as the organizers cast it—all focusing on the impact of a person's faith in both public and private life. The event is nonpartisan and attendance is by invitation only. Participants include elected and appointed officials from virtually every branch and level of government, as well as heads of state, ambassadors, and representatives from numerous other countries. A limited number of men and women from other walks of life, such as business and education, also take part. Over the years I've had several opportunities to be present.

Once I remember sitting at a table with an older gentlemen who was a veteran of many National Prayer Breakfasts. After what he thought was the opening course of assorted breads and fruit, he was ready for the "real" food—eggs, bacon, and other more substantial fare. Since he last attended, however, the menu had been scaled back, probably to keep costs down. Even after the program began, he continued repeating the question, louder and louder each time, "Where's the rest of breakfast? Where's the REST of breakfast? WHERE'S THE REST OF BREAKFAST?"

Security for this event is always heavy, and I became increasingly concerned that police officers were going to come and evict him. Finally, I think someone offered him another roll (or stuffed it in his mouth), and he quieted down.

For many attendees, the high point of the breakfast comes when the president of the United States is announced and enters the room. The air suddenly seems rarefied. As he takes his seat at the head table with other speakers and musicians who are on the program, he becomes the focus of every eye. It's gratifying that, in the midst of all the pressing affairs of state confronting him, the leader of the free world makes an event devoted to prayer his priority, at least for an hour or so.

In the face of the work confronting Him, Christ made prayer—communion with His heavenly Father—His ongoing priority. Luke records, "Jesus Himself would often slip away to the wilderness and pray" (Luke 5:16). He would also pray instantaneously, on the spot. Prayer was so prominent in His life that those closest to Him, the disciples, made it the subject of an explicit request.

"Lord," they said, "teach us to pray" (Luke 11:1).

Judging by the sheer number of books that have been written on this subject, it's easy to imagine that Christ might have responded by delivering to them an extended series of lengthy lectures. That's not what the Scripture tells us. Rather, Jesus replied with profound simplicity.

"When you are praying," He told them, "do not use meaningless repetition as the Gentiles do, for they suppose that they will be heard for their many words. So do not be like them; for your Father knows what you need before you ask Him." Jesus then taught how to pray:

> Pray, then, in this way: "Our Father who is in heaven, hallowed be Your name. Your kingdom come Your will be done, on earth as it is in heaven. Give us this day our daily bread. And forgive us our debts, as we also have forgiven our debtors. And do not lead us into temptation, but deliver us from evil. For Yours is the kingdom and the power and the glory forever. Amen" (Matthew 6:7-13).

Jesus especially underscored to the disciples the necessity of praying with a forgiving heart: "If you forgive others for their transgressions, your heavenly Father will also forgive you. But if you do not forgive others, then your Father will not forgive your transgressions" (Matthew 6:14-15).

Among other aspects of prayer, Jesus also emphasized the willingness—indeed, the eagerness—of the heavenly Father to respond to persistent, expectant prayer.

> Suppose one of you has a friend, and goes to him at midnight and says to him, "Friend, lend me three loaves; for a friend of mine has come to me from a journey, and I have nothing to set before him"; and from inside he answers and says, "Do not bother me; the door has already been shut and my children and I are in bed; I cannot get up and give you anything."
>
> I tell you, even though he will not get up and give him anything because he is his friend, yet because of his persistence he will get up and give him as much as he needs. So I say to you, ask, and it will be given to you; seek, and you will find; knock, and it will be opened to you. For everyone who asks, receives; and he who seeks, finds; and to him who knocks, it will be opened (Luke 11:5-10).

Relatively few people today, even among Christians, are willing to testify to the vibrancy of their own personal prayer life. Prayer is probably the most over-discussed, under-practiced aspect of Christian living. (I'd also say that evangelism—telling others the good news of Christ and inviting them to repent of their sins and believe in Him—is the most under-discussed, under-practiced aspect.) This is particularly true in America and other developed societies, where we have so many pursuits to keep us busy and distract us and where it's so easy for us to think that we're self-sufficient and don't need God.[8]

For the Son of God, however, prayer wasn't optional; it was essential. It wasn't just some daily ritual for Him, either. He lived to pray and He prayed in order to live—purposefully, in a fallen, sin-sick world, for His Father's glory. If Jesus did that, how much more do we need to do so!

My prayer life has a long way to go. Sure, I pray regularly and I pray multiple times during the day. I'm typically awake by 4:30 or 5:00 a.m. and usually spend that early morning time praying and reading Scripture. I pray sitting, standing, kneeling, and prone (sometimes when I do that I fall back asleep!). I also pray most anywhere I happen to be.

Prayer is, for me, much more than just asking God for things. Because I am not sinless, I often need to confess my sins to God and receive His forgiveness and cleansing. Prayer for me also involves quiet waiting before the Lord as well expressions of gratitude and adoration. And sometimes when I pray, exultation wells up in my soul and causes me to sing and dance before the Lord (if that seems foolish, the Bible says in 2 Samuel 6 that King David did it too).

I pray for God's guidance; I pray for strength and protection; I pray for the needs of my loved ones; I pray for those who seek to do me ill; I pray for government leaders and world affairs; I pray for missionaries and pastors and churches; I pray for the salvation of people who have not yet received Christ. Sometimes, when it's a key issue in my schedule, I even pray for a parking place!

But despite it all, my focus on the Lord is too easily diverted by the seemingly urgent matters of life…and, of course, Satan delights in disrupting our communion with God. At times I lose sight of the fact that, apart from Him, I can't do anything of heavenly quality or eternal significance. One of my prayers is to pray better, to pray more richly, to pray with greater effectiveness. Please pray with me to that end!

Nothing could interrupt Jesus' fellowship with His Father. Still, He often retreated from His disciples and from the crowds that followed Him in order to have concentrated times of prayer. And His time in the wilderness, after being baptized by John, was a prolonged season of prayer that prepared Him for the work ahead of Him…work that no one had done before, work that no one—not any president, prime minister, or other earthly potentate—will ever be able to do: the work of making forgiveness, salvation, and eternal life available to the world.

And oh…about the National Prayer Breakfast: I must say, with all due respect, that the president's entrance really isn't the high point of the time. That moment comes when all who trust in the Lord Jesus Christ invoke His name and by faith enter the very throne room of Almighty God in prayer. That's a privilege available to us not just one day a year in a specific setting, but every moment of every day wherever we are and whatever we're doing. It's also something Christ urged His followers to do in view of the perils at hand.

"Pray," He said, "that you may not enter into temptation" (Luke 22:40).

He knew from personal experience what He was talking about.

Draw Near and Be Transformed

How consistently do you pray, and how important would the people who know you best say that prayer is to you?

Do you feel like you have to use special words in your prayers or are you comfortable using everyday language when you talk to God?

Do you think of prayer as primarily asking God to give you something you want, or do you think of it as a way of giving yourself to God to use for His purposes?

Could your prayers be hindered because you're harboring a grudge toward someone you think has done you wrong? Is it more important to you to continue nursing your anger, or to be in fellowship with God?

Do you think of God as being eager to bless you? Why or why not?

Of all the things you pray for, have you ever considered that the Person of Jesus Christ Himself is the real answer to your prayers?

In what ways would you like for your experience of prayer to grow?

12

Tempted

*He was in the wilderness forty days being
tempted by Satan; and He was with the wild
beasts, and the angels were ministering to Him.*

MARK 1:13

God has one Son without sin—He has no
children who haven't been tempted.

The first visitors to the region knew it mostly just for its sunbaked sand. Only about four or five inches of rain fell per year. Insects crawled and buzzed and flew in their perpetual quest to annoy something or somebody. Lizards, scorpions, and tarantulas all found their own ways to survive. Here and there a snake would lie in wait for some hapless rodent to wander by, which would promptly become its entrée of the day. Mountain lions stalked their prey; coyotes often settled for the lions' leftovers. Early explorers referred to the route through the valley as "the journey of death."

One day, however, a scout looking for water in the parched desert came upon a spring flowing from the earth. The spring provided respite from the triple-digit heat and, around it, grasses and other vegetation flourished. Soon afterward a settlement sprang up. It served as a welcome oasis for travelers.

Over the decades, fed by the comings and goings of stagecoaches, trains, and eventually automobiles and airplanes, and amidst the usual assemblage of homes, shops, and churches that comprise a community, something else sprang up too. Its development was driven by ambitious entrepreneurs as well as ruthless mobsters. Profiting by offering passing pleasures that were illegal most elsewhere—gambling, illicit sex, free-flowing booze, and drugs—they built what's known today as The Strip…Glitter Gulch…Sin City…Las Vegas.

Even in recent times the entertainment industry in Las Vegas has marketed itself with the line, "What happens here stays here," suggesting that there are no lasting consequences to casting off restraint and going on a binge of self-indulgence there. Somehow their ads omit the fact that the suicide rate in Las Vegas is roughly four times higher than it is in nongaming communities and that the city scores poorly in measures of a host of other social ills. As Moses declared to the children of Israel, "Be sure your sin will find you out" (Numbers 32:23).[9]

Someone has said that "the only trouble with resisting temptation is that you may not get another chance." Las Vegas is a city that has boomed based on both temptation and chance. It's a place where many live by the words of one moral degenerate who said, "the only way to get rid of temptation is to yield to it.… I can resist everything but temptation."

It may surprise you, but Jesus Himself faced the challenge of resisting temptation. A pivotal episode occurred in the wilderness after He was baptized. When "He had fasted forty days and forty nights, He then became hungry. And the tempter came and said to Him, 'If You are the Son of God, command that these stones become bread'" (Matthew 4:2-3).

> But He answered and said, "It is written, 'Man shall not live on bread alone, but on every word that proceeds out of the mouth of God.'"
>
> Then the devil took Him into the holy city and had Him stand on the pinnacle of the temple, and said to Him, "If You are the Son of God, throw Yourself down; for it is

written, 'He will command His angels concerning You'; and 'On their hands they will bear You up, so that You will not strike Your foot against a stone.'" Jesus said to him, "On the other hand, it is written, 'You shall not put the Lord your God to the test.'"

Again, the devil took Him to a very high mountain and showed Him all the kingdoms of the world and their glory; and he said to Him, "All these things I will give You, if You fall down and worship me." Then Jesus said to him, "Go, Satan! For it is written, 'You shall worship the Lord your God, and serve Him only.'" Then the devil left Him; and behold, angels came and began to minister to Him (Matthew 4:4-11).

In this duel with the devil, Christ demonstrated that being tempted does not in itself constitute sin, for He, the Son of God Himself, was tempted yet remained sinless. God has one Son without sin—He has no children who haven't been tempted. (Satan even twisted and misused Scripture in his attempt to lure Jesus!) Our problem is that we step over the line into sin when we court and indulge temptation rather than resisting and overcoming it.

The great British writer C.S. Lewis said, "A silly idea is current that good people do not know what temptation means. This is an obvious lie. Only those who try to resist temptation know how strong it is…. A man who gives in to temptation after five minutes simply does not know what it would have been like an hour later. That is why bad people, in one sense, know very little about badness. They have lived a sheltered life by always giving in."[10]

Christ, however, never gave in; at every turn He confuted the tempter by accurately wielding the truth of God's Word in response to the devil's enticing lies. You see, temptation always has, at its core, a lie. Jesus said of Satan, "He was a murderer from the beginning, and does not stand in the truth because there is no truth in him. Whenever he speaks a lie, he speaks from his own nature, for he is a liar and the father of lies" (John 8:44).

To Adam and Eve and to all of us, Satan's lie is that we can be like God without God, that we can experience His choice blessings through our own efforts and apart from trust in and obedience to Him. Satan fans the flame of temptation with the notion that God, in giving us commandments and boundaries, is depriving us of something good and that we really owe it to ourselves to seize it and enjoy it. Satan is a master at presenting his enticements in glittery wrapping that obscures the bitterness they'll ultimately bring us. He whispers words of rationalization that in reality beckon us to destruction. As any resolve we have starts to melt, he eggs us on with urgency, never inkling that his aim is, in the words of Jesus, "to steal and kill and destroy" (John 10:10). In the end, by succumbing to temptation, what we really do is turn our backs on the God who made us, loves us with an everlasting love, and wants the very best for us. The result, according to Christ, is bondage.

"Truly, truly, I say to you," He said, "everyone who commits sin is the slave of sin" (John 8:34).

Jesus, however, saw through the devil's lies and remained ever faithful to His Father. Remaining faithful in the wilderness when He was "about thirty years of age" (Luke 3:23) was preparation for remaining faithful through the temptations that would come to Him in the course of His ministry and would culminate three years later at the cross. In doing so, He became the greatest Friend of all who are tempted. "We do not have a high priest," the Bible says in Hebrews 2:17, "who cannot sympathize with our weaknesses, but One who has been tempted in all things as we are, yet without sin."

Christ faced and resisted temptations to indulge the lust of the flesh, the pride of life, and the lust of the eyes, all of which the Bible says are part of this current world system that is passing away. He knew that "the one who does the will of God lives forever" (1 John 2:17). And now, "since He Himself was tempted in that which He has suffered, He is able to come to the aid of those who are tempted" (Hebrews 2:18).

In fact, in Christ we have some wonderfully freeing promises. One is that when we trust Christ and have the Holy Spirit living in our hearts, we don't have to sin: "No temptation has overtaken you but such as is common to man; and God is faithful, who will not allow you to be tempted beyond what you are able, but with the temptation will provide the way of escape also, so that you will be able to endure it" (1 Corinthians 10:13).

Another is that, when we do succumb to temptation, Christ Himself acts not as our accuser but as our Advocate with the Father (see 1 John 2:1), and God offers us forgiveness and cleansing from sin because of Him: "If we confess our sins, He is faithful and righteous to forgive us our sins and to cleanse us from all unrighteousness" (1 John 1:9).

"Therefore," the Bible urges us, "let us draw near with confidence to the throne of grace, so that we may receive mercy and find grace to help in time of need" (Hebrews 4:16).

Such merciful, gracious help is available to us because Christ was faithful even when He was tempted. It's worth noting as well that His Father was also faithful to Him. After Jesus' struggle with the tempter, God sent angels to minister to Him.

Many unbiblical and even silly notions about angels abound in our day. Angels are presented in Scripture as mighty spirit-beings created by God to do His bidding. They protect and minister to people, implement God's plans, and, at times, execute His judgment. Satan himself was originally an angel who led an uprising of other angels against God and who, with them, was cast out of heaven.[11] Even now the agenda of the devil and his fallen angels, also called demons, is to oppose the purposes of God.

But neither an angel nor a demon is like God: all-powerful, all-knowing, or everywhere-present. On this day in the wilderness the devil lost, Jesus triumphed, and all who trust Him gained in the process. Not even the wild animals—at odds with the human race since Adam and Eve fell—had a quarrel with the righteous Son of God.

As Jesus went forth from the wilderness, multitudes were waiting to hear what He had to say. They had never heard anything like it.

DRAW NEAR AND BE TRANSFORMED

How do you respond to the notion that "there are no lasting consequences to casting off restraint and going on a binge of self-indulgence"?

Do you tend to think of being tempted as sin? Does Jesus' experience change that perspective for you?

What do you learn from the way Jesus responded to the tempter? How does the idea that He is "the greatest Friend of all who are tempted" affect your view of Him?

The Bible says, "Each one is tempted when he is carried away and enticed by his own lust" (James 1:14). How can you improve your ability to see through and overcome temptation?

Spend time right now acknowledging your particular sins to God and thanking Him for His provision of forgiveness and cleansing, as expressed in 1 John 1:9, for all who trust in Chist.

Teaching

*They were amazed at His teaching; for He was
teaching them as one having authority...*

MARK 1:22

Christ had no doubts about His message because
He *was* the Word of God in human flesh.

The young preacher was in a quandary. While searching for
direction about what shape his developing work should take, his
plight was aggravated by the fact that a friend in ministry was now
having serious questions about his faith, especially about the Scriptures. He had to admit to himself that he, too, was having similar
questions. After all, popular writers of the day were making assertions that didn't square with what he had been taught as a child
and learned while he was in school. At the heart of his dilemma was
whether the Bible could be trusted. His struggle left him feeling
hypocritical. He could not go on preaching to people while, at
the same time, having nagging doubts in his own mind about the
Bible's reliability. With an ever-busier schedule looming before him,
something had to give. He had to resolve the issue one way or the
other, once and for all.

One moonlit night he went for a walk in the woods, pondering the questions swirling in his head. As he related years later:

> Dropping to my knees there in the woods, I opened the Bible at random on a tree stump in front of me. I could not read it in the shadowy moonlight, so I had no idea what text lay before me...I could only stutter into prayer. The exact wording of my prayer is beyond recall, but it must have echoed my thoughts: "O God! There are many things in this book I do not understand. There are many problems with it for which I have no solution. There are many seeming contradictions. There are some areas in it that do not seem to correlate with modern science. I can't answer some of the philosophical and psychological questions..."

Then this young preacher made a commitment that would forever mark his life.

"Father, I am going to accept this as Thy Word—by *faith!* I'm going to allow faith to go beyond my intellectual questions and doubts, and I will believe this to be your inspired Word."

Reflecting on that moment, he said, "When I got up from my knees, I sensed the presence and power of God as I had not sensed it in months. Not all my questions were answered, but a major bridge had been crossed. In my heart and mind, I knew a spiritual battle had been fought and won." Throughout his subsequent ministry, people would comment on the conviction and authority with which he preached.[12]

When Christ began teaching the crowds that thronged after Him, He spoke with unparalleled conviction and authority. He had no doubts about His message because He *was* the Word of God in human flesh. One of the 12 men Jesus chose to be with Him as His disciples, a fisherman named John, began his Gospel account about Jesus by saying, "In the beginning was the Word, and the Word was with God, and the Word was God. He was in the beginning with God" (John 1:1-2).

Jesus Himself told His hearers, "You search the Scriptures…it is these that testify about Me" (John 5:39). And, in the words of one of the New Testament writers, "God, after He spoke long ago to the fathers in the prophets in many portions and in many ways, in these last days has spoken to us in His Son…. And He is…the exact representation of His nature" (Hebrews 1:1-3).

The authority in Christ's words was evident to those who heard Him. After being tempted

> He came to Nazareth, where He had been brought up; and as was His custom, He entered the synagogue on the Sabbath, and stood up to read. And the book of the prophet Isaiah was handed to Him. And He opened the book and found the place where it was written, "The Spirit of the Lord is upon Me, because He anointed Me to preach the gospel to the poor. He has sent Me to proclaim release to the captives, and recovery of sight to the blind, to set free those who are oppressed, to proclaim the favorable year of the Lord."
>
> And He closed the book, gave it back to the attendant and sat down; and the eyes of all in the synagogue were fixed on Him. And He began to say to them, "Today this Scripture has been fulfilled in your hearing." And all were speaking well of Him, and wondering at the gracious words which were falling from His lips (Luke 4:16-22).

In response to this keynote message of His ministry, as well as to His subsequent teaching, people were "amazed…for He was teaching them as one having authority, and not as the scribes" (Mark 1:22).

As Christ spoke, people wrestled in their minds to come to terms with what He was saying. "Teacher," one man asked, "which is the great commandment in the Law?"

> He said to him, "You shall love the Lord your God with all your heart, and with all your soul, and with all your mind." This is the great and foremost commandment. The second is like it, "You shall love your neighbor as yourself. On these two commandments depend the whole Law and the Prophets" (Matthew 22:36-40).

As Jesus proclaimed the Word of God, He unfolded its meaning with a power that penetrated people's hearts. His Sermon on the Mount, for example, recorded in the Gospel according to Matthew—a tax collector also chosen by Jesus to be one of the Twelve—magnified the demands of the Great Commandment with specific applications that pierced external, superficial morality. Far from being a way of salvation, properly understood, the Sermon on the Mount drives us to our knees with an acute realization of our desperate need for Christ's salvation.

The result of Jesus' teaching was that people were astonished. "Never has a man spoken the way this man speaks," they declared (John 7:46).

That's all well and good, you may say, but I've never heard Christ speak. All I have to go on today is the Bible and, like that young preacher, I have lots of questions about it. Is it indeed reliable? Is it, as one historic creed declares, "the only infallible rule of faith and practice"?

My response is that, like that young preacher, each of us ultimately does have to accept the Bible by faith. Doing so, however, does not require blind, irrational faith. To the contrary, it's quite reasonable. It's a leap not into the dark but, rather, into the light.

The Bible we have today that has been translated and passed down from generation to generation is supported by a greater quantity of historical manuscripts—and demonstrates a greater degree of textual consistency and fidelity—than any other ancient document.

The Dead Sea scrolls provide some of the earliest corroboration of the accuracy of the Old Testament manuscripts that served as the basis for today's translations.

Christ Himself affirmed the inspiration and integrity of the Old Testament, which were the Scriptures in existence while He was here. The New Testament was written within the lifetime of eyewitnesses to Christ's life and ministry, by apostles and others whose work could have been decisively refuted had it been untrue.

And archaeology has repeatedly verified key portions of both the Old and New Testaments. When thoroughly considered, there is more evidence for the reliability of the Bible than other sources of information on which we make decisions and take action every day!

It really comes down to a question of our premise: Could Almighty God, in choosing to reveal Himself to the human race, inspire and superintend the compilation of a cohesive and accurate written record of His nature, ways, and will, or would imparting and preserving such a record be too difficult for Him? From my perspective—in an age when billions of bits of information are routinely stored on silicon microchips—while the Bible is certainly a wonder, producing it was for God (I say this reverently) no big deal. For most people, I think their difficulty in accepting the Bible was summed up by Mark Twain when he said, "It ain't those parts of the Bible that I can't understand that bother me—it's the parts that I do understand."

Many of Christ's hearers, especially the religious leaders, were greatly troubled by both what they did understand in His teaching as well as what they didn't. Jesus, perceiving in some the attitude that His talk could be just empty words, gave them even more to talk about—namely, His amazing works. Those works would leave them, in today's vernacular, unable to compute.

And, oh, who was that young preacher who determined that night in the woods to rely on the Scriptures? Just the man God would use to preach the gospel of Christ to more people than anyone else in history—Billy Graham. And his commitment to the

Scriptures endured throughout his life, a fact to which he testi-
fied in the book he authored as his legacy for Christian living, *The
Journey,* and published in his late eighties. There, in reflecting on
his moment of commitment to the Scriptures so many years earlier,
he wrote these uncompromising words:

> Especially significant to me...was Jesus' own view of
> Scripture. He not only quoted it frequently, but also
> accepted it as the Word of God.... He also told [His
> disciples], "I tell you the truth, until heaven and earth
> disappear, not the smallest letter, not the least stroke of
> a pen [rendered in some Bible translations as "jot" and
> "tittle," referring to markings in the Hebrew alphabet],
> will by any means disappear from the Law."...Shouldn't
> I have the same view of Scripture as my Lord?[13]

DRAW NEAR AND BE TRANSFORMED

Do you approach the Bible with the premise that it is God's reliable, authoritative Word, or do you think imparting and preserving such a record would be too difficult for Him? Why?

What parts of the Bible bother you the most? What are you doing about the parts you do understand?

How would determining once and for all to embrace the Bible as "the only infallible rule of faith and practice" affect your life? Why not take that step right now?

14

Working

Truly, truly, I say to you, the Son can do nothing of Himself, unless it is something He sees the Father doing; for whatever the Father does, these things the Son also does in like manner.

JOHN 5:19

Jesus wasn't some wandering magician dazzling people with capricious signs and wonders—His works validated His uniqueness as God's only begotten Son.

Our son Gregory has always been a good worker. He can do many things well. As I write, he's guiding a group on a backpacking expedition in the mountains. Graduating from college with a focus on wilderness leadership, he's more comfortable sleeping in a tent in a national forest than he is in a bed in the city. He and his brother Nathan and I have done enough of the former together for me to know that, most of the time, I prefer the latter!

Gregory is also experienced at rafting and kayaking and has spent several summers guiding groups down rivers in the American West as well as in Central America. Getting paid to explore places such as the Teton Mountains, Yellowstone National Park, and Jackson Hole, Wyoming, is a rough way to make a living!

When he isn't in the woods somewhere, Gregory can often be found making things with wood. A high school carpentry class he took eventually led him to develop his abilities as a finish carpenter, a trade with which he has been able to support himself. Though I seldom have time to do much of it, I too enjoy carpentry—my paternal grandfather was a carpenter. (And the Lord Jesus Himself learned carpentry from Joseph.) I admire the grains and hues of wood and enjoy the aromas of pine and cedar and oak and walnut— what an amazing substance God created!

Gregory's first occupation, however, was lawn maintenance. He was three. He had a little plastic red-and-yellow mower that made a clicking sound when it rolled. Whenever I set out to cut our grass with my adult-size push mower he would follow along, carefully walking row-by-row in my footsteps until "we" had mowed the entire lawn. As far as he was concerned, the only difference between his lawn mower and mine was that mine required real gasoline and his didn't. He relished, though, doing exactly what his father did. The Lord Jesus approached His ministry the same way.

One day some Jews were objecting to the fact that Jesus healed people on the Sabbath.

"Truly, truly, I say to you," He told them, "the Son can do nothing of Himself, unless it is something He sees the Father doing; for whatever the Father does, these things the Son also does in like manner" (John 5:19).

During the course of His ministry, the Son did quite a lot of extraordinary things—so many that John concluded his Gospel account by noting:

> Therefore many other signs Jesus also performed in the presence of the disciples, which are not written in this book; but these have been written so that you may believe that Jesus is the Christ, the Son of God; and that

believing you may have life in His name.... And there are also many other things which Jesus did, which if they were written in detail, I suppose that even the world itself would not contain the books that would be written (John 20:30-31; 21:25).

In fact, Christ had been working since before the world came into being. Gospel writer John says that "all things came into being through Him, and apart from Him nothing came into being that has come into being" (John 1:3). When God spoke creation into being from nothing, the Son was integral in the process.

Scripture records for us more than 30 miracles Jesus performed during His earthly ministry—actual, literal acts of power attributable only to divine intervention in the normal course of human affairs that altered the expected outcome. These included...

- turning water into wine at a wedding in Cana, labeled the "beginning of His signs" (John 2:11) and ruling out spurious fables about His childhood activities;

- healing and cleansing numerous individuals of a variety of physical afflictions, including blindness, deafness, paralysis, epilepsy, and leprosy;

- astonishing the disciples, some of whom were professional fishermen, with catches of fish so great they could scarcely manage them;

- delivering demon-possessed individuals from the dark powers of hell enslaving them;

- raising people from the dead on three separate occasions;

- feeding multitudes numbering in the thousands on two occasions, starting with just a little bread and fish and ending up with plenty remaining;

- walking on water and calming the stormy Sea of Galilee; and

- cursing a fig tree—a symbol for Israel—that didn't bear fruit and causing it to wither.

These were not random, whimsical events. Jesus wasn't some wandering magician amusing and dazzling people with capricious signs and wonders. To the contrary, each of His works brought glory to His Father, validated His uniqueness as the only begotten Son of God, and summoned people to believe in Him: "The works which the Father has given Me to accomplish—the very works that I do—testify about Me, that the Father has sent Me" (John 5:36).

Jesus went on to say,

> Do you not believe that I am in the Father, and the Father is in Me? The words that I say to you I do not speak on My own initiative, but the Father abiding in Me does His works. Believe Me that I am in the Father and the Father is in Me; otherwise believe because of the works themselves (John 14:10-11).

And ultimately, all Christ's works were stepping stones toward the Great Work for which He came—paying the penalty for sin on the cross in order to deliver us from our futile attempts to become right with God through our own inadequate works.

"What shall we do, so that we may work the works of God?" His hearers asked Him one day. Jesus answered and said, "This is the work of God, that you believe in Him whom He has sent" (John 6:28-29).

That's why the apostle Paul wrote to believers in Christ living in Ephesus, "By grace you have been saved through faith; and that not of yourselves, it is the gift of God; not as a result of works, so that no one may boast" (Ephesians 2:8-9). That's why he wrote to Christians in Galatia, "A man is not justified by the works of the Law but through faith in Christ Jesus...by the works of the Law no flesh will be justified" (Galatians 2:16).

While many marveled at Jesus' works, others—including

members of His own family—were offended by them. In response Jesus simply said, "If I do not do the works of My Father, do not believe Me; but if I do them, though you do not believe Me, believe the works, so that you may know and understand that the Father is in Me, and I in the Father" (John 10:37-38).

His Father's assignment for His life was ever His priority and focus: "My food is to do the will of Him who sent Me and to accomplish His work" (John 4:34).

And as Jesus would demonstrate, *how* one works is just as important as what he does.

DRAW NEAR AND BE TRANSFORMED

How do you react to the idea that Jesus performed miracles—actual, literal acts of power attributable only to divine intervention in the normal course of human affairs that altered the expected outcome?

Do you agree or disagree that these miracles validated His uniqueness as the only begotten Son of God and summoned people to believe in Him? Why?

Would you say that, instead of relying on "the Great Work for which He came—paying the penalty for sin on the cross," that you're still engaged in attempting to have right standing with God through your own works? How are you doing at measuring up to the perfect standard of Christ's life?

To what extent is doing God's will more important to you than anything else—even food?

15

Serving

For even the Son of Man did not come to be served,
but to serve, and to give His life a ransom for many.

MARK 10:45

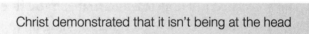

Christ demonstrated that it isn't being at the head
of things that matters—it's being at the foot.

Saddam Hussein—the very mention of his name evokes images
of a mercurial tyrant who maintained power over the people of
Iraq (which in ancient times was Babylon) through intimidation
and brutality, while, at the same time, living personally in opulent
splendor.

An observer of just one of Hussein's multiple palaces described it
as having "more than 40 incredibly ornate buildings" inside a com-
pound occupying more than ten square miles along the Tigris River.
Each structure had "a different sandstone exterior with elaborate
Arabic designs." Floors were "all marble and the furnishings were
very detailed, although somewhat gaudy."[14] Born in a house of mud,
he had developed a lifestyle for himself in which he had alcohol,
fresh steaks, and seafood flown in twice a week, and enjoyed British
chocolates. Though married, he reportedly had sexual relationships

with other women. All the while, he regularly pored over reports from his secret police, looking with paranoia for the slightest threat. For any indication, either real or imagined, of possible treason, he ordered executions. He murdered not only on an individual scale but on a larger one as well, using chemical weapons to kill thousands of his subjects.

In time, on April 9, 2003, a coalition of Western military forces led by the United States toppled Hussein's self-centered regime. When he could no longer hold on to power, he fled for his life. Eventually the man who had come to be known as the butcher of Baghdad was found hiding in a hole in the ground. How the mighty had fallen!

What a different ruler Christ showed Himself to be! "For even the Son of Man did not come to be served, but to serve," He declared, "and to give His life a ransom for many" (Mark 10:45). And He not only declared it, He also demonstrated it to His disciples. One day, for example, "they were on the road going up to Jerusalem" (Mark 10:32). Let's look at what happened:

> Jesus was walking on ahead of them; and they were amazed, and those who followed were fearful. And again He took the twelve aside and began to tell them what was going to happen to Him, saying, "Behold, we are going up to Jerusalem, and the Son of Man will be delivered to the chief priests and the scribes; and they will condemn Him to death and will hand Him over to the Gentiles. They will mock Him and spit on Him, and scourge Him and kill Him, and three days later He will rise again" (verses 32-34).

Somehow, the disciples seemed to miss His message:

> James and John, the two sons of Zebedee, came up to Jesus, saying, "Teacher, we want You to do for us whatever we ask of You." And He said to them, "What do you want Me to do for you?" They said to Him, "Grant that

we may sit, one on Your right and one on Your left, in Your glory." But Jesus said to them, "You do not know what you are asking. Are you able to drink the cup that I drink, or to be baptized with the baptism with which I am baptized?" They said to Him, "We are able." And Jesus said to them, "The cup that I drink you shall drink; and you shall be baptized with the baptism with which I am baptized. But to sit on My right or on My left, this is not Mine to give; but it is for those for whom it has been prepared."

Do you know the feeling you get when you're standing in line at the airport or in a restaurant or crowded store and somebody elbows his way in front of you? I think the other disciples must have felt like James and John had just elbowed them. You can almost see the hair on the back of their necks standing up in indignation. Jesus, however, saw this as a teachable moment.

Hearing this, the ten began to feel indignant with James and John. Calling them to Himself, Jesus said to them, "You know that those who are recognized as rulers of the Gentiles lord it over them; and their great men exercise authority over them. But it is not this way among you, but whoever wishes to become great among you shall be your servant; and whoever wishes to be first among you shall be slave of all" (Mark 10:32-44).

I'd venture to guess that those piercing words were not what the disciples wanted to hear. After all, they really do turn this world's order—where the prevailing rule is often "eat or be eaten"—on its head. Christ went on, however, to demonstrate that it isn't being at the head of things that matters—it's being at the foot.

On the night before He died,

Jesus, knowing that the Father had given all things into His hands, and that He had come forth from God and was going back to God, got up from supper, and laid aside His garments; and taking a towel, He girded Himself. Then He poured water into the basin, and began to wash the disciples' feet and to wipe them with the towel with which He was girded. So He came to Simon Peter. He said to Him, "Lord, do You wash my feet?" Jesus answered and said to him, "What I do you do not realize now, but you will understand hereafter."...

So when He had washed their feet, and taken His garments and reclined at the table again, He said to them, "Do you know what I have done to you? You call Me Teacher and Lord; and you are right, for so I am. If I then, the Lord and the Teacher, washed your feet, you also ought to wash one another's feet. For I gave you an example that you also should do as I did to you. Truly, truly, I say to you, a slave is not greater than his master, nor is one who is sent greater than the one who sent him. If you know these things, you are blessed if you do them" (John 13:3-7,12-17).

As Jesus words' hung in the air, I imagine that, for a moment, the disciples forgot to breathe. Some must have fidgeted; others must have squirmed. In their minds they were likely trying to picture themselves doing what Jesus had just done. Looking around the table at one another they may have been thinking, *Well...I might do it to this one but, to that one? No way.*

Yet Christ had spoken, and He had acted. Like it or not, His example was right there in front of them like the dishes on the table. What He had done and said would play over and over again in their minds for the rest of their days. Till the day they died they would live and serve with the truth before them that "the high and exalted One who lives forever, whose name is Holy" dwells "with the contrite and lowly of spirit" (Isaiah 57:15). They would be forever marked by "the grace of our Lord Jesus Christ" who "though He was rich, yet for your sake He became poor, so that you through His poverty might become rich" (2 Corinthians 8:9).

For people who by nature were self-seeking rather than others-serving, they no doubt found that serving one another could be hard work—so hard, in fact, that at times their greatest need was just to get some rest. Jesus knew about that, too.

DRAW NEAR AND BE TRANSFORMED

How do you react when somebody elbows his way in front of you, either literally or figurative, whether at home or work or in your dealings in the world?

In what ways do you struggle with Christ's teaching that true greatness and leadership consist of servanthood?

Does it stun you that the Son of God Himself would assume the posture and role of a slave, then tell His followers to do the same? Have you embraced that call in your life? How are you living it out?

Jesus said that those who serve are blessed. Pause right now and ask God to help you experience more of His presence as the One who dwells "with the contrite and lowly of spirit."

So the Son of Man is Lord even of the Sabbath.

MARK 2:28

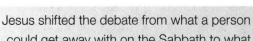

Jesus shifted the debate from what a person
could get away with on the Sabbath to what
kind of focus makes the Sabbath truly holy.

"It was the best business decision we ever made."

The person who spoke those words had grown up in America's
Great Depression and learned early to work hard in order to survive.
For income, his parents rented rooms in their house to boarders,
and their whole family took part in preparing meals, washing the
dishes, and doing the laundry. As a young man just after World
War II ended, he and his brother scraped together a few thousand
dollars and opened a 24-hour diner. It had four tables and ten stools;
receipts from their first day of operation totaled $58.20.

Despite this small beginning his business grew, driven by his
strong work ethic that had been forged in the fires of his childhood hardship. Along the way he experimented with his menu and
developed a sandwich recipe that he at first licensed to others, and
then decided to use as the core of his own new restaurant concept.

He also made the decision to open a store within a retailing revolution that was just beginning—a shopping mall. When that location proved profitable, he opened another one, then another, and another. Today, his restaurants number over 1200 and they're spread across three-quarters of the American landscape.

What was that "best business decision" this man made? Was it operating 24 hours a day when he first started out? Was it developing his special sandwich? Was it making his food available to customers in shopping malls? Not any of these.

It was, he said, deciding at the end of his first week of business that they would be closed on Sundays.

To some that sounded crazy. Why in the world would he give up the potential profit of one day out of every seven when he had a fledgling restaurant?

His answer: "Our decision to close on Sunday was our way of honoring God and directing our attention to things more important than our business. If it took seven days to make a living with a restaurant, then we needed to be in some other line of work."

A follower of Christ since the age of 12, he wanted to make sure that he and his family, as well as those working with him, had the chance to worship and rest. The decision certainly paid off. Today, Truett Cathy's Chik-fil-A restaurants ring up about two billion dollars in annual sales. Not a bad return for working six days out of seven!

Jesus knew the importance of rest. He was, after all, there in the beginning when "the heavens and the earth were completed, and all their hosts" (Genesis 2:1). The Scripture goes on to say:

> By the seventh day God completed His work which He had done, and He rested on the seventh day from all His work which He had done. Then God blessed the seventh day and sanctified it, because in it He rested from all His work which God had created and made (Genesis 2:2-3).

Christ was there when God gave Moses the Ten Commandments on Mount Sinai. In the commandments, God said,

> Remember the sabbath day, to keep it holy. Six days you shall labor and do all your work, but the seventh day is a sabbath of the LORD your God; in it you shall not do any work, you or your son or your daughter, your male or your female servant or your cattle or your sojourner who stays with you. For in six days the LORD made the heavens and the earth, the sea and all that is in them, and rested on the seventh day; therefore the LORD blessed the sabbath day and made it holy (Exodus 20:8-11).

Jesus, during His ministry on earth, planted the flag of His Lordship squarely in the midst of the Sabbath. "The Sabbath was made for man, and not man for the Sabbath," He declared. "So the Son of Man is Lord even of the Sabbath" (Mark 2:27).

Over and over again in the Old Testament, properly observing the Sabbath was a point of stumbling and disobedience for Israel, one for which they were repeatedly rebuked and chastened. In fact, by the time Jesus appeared, the Jewish leaders had taken something that God intended as a blessing for His people and turned it into a burden. They had developed their own elaborate rules that focused more on legalistically parsing out what a person could get away with on the Sabbath than on honoring the One who had established it.

That's why, for example, they contended with Jesus when

> on another Sabbath He entered the synagogue and was teaching; and there was a man there whose right hand was withered. The scribes and the Pharisees were watching Him closely to see if He healed on the Sabbath, so that they might find reason to accuse Him. But He knew what they were thinking, and He said to the man with the withered hand, "Get up and come forward!" And he got up and came forward. And Jesus said to them, "I ask you, is it lawful to do good or to do harm on the Sabbath,

to save a life or to destroy it?" After looking around at them all, He said to him, "Stretch out your hand!" And he did so; and his hand was restored. But they themselves were filled with rage, and discussed together what they might do to Jesus. It was at this time that He went off to the mountain to pray, and He spent the whole night in prayer to God" (Luke 6:6-12).

On another Sabbath, Jesus healed "a woman who for eighteen years had had a sickness caused by a spirit; and she was bent double, and could not straighten up at all." When an indignant synagogue official challenged His action, Jesus said,

> You hypocrites, does not each of you on the Sabbath untie his ox or his donkey from the stall and lead him away to water him? And this woman, a daughter of Abraham as she is, whom Satan has bound for eighteen long years, should she not have been released from this bond on the Sabbath day? (Luke 13:11,15-16).

Scripture says that all Jesus' opponents were being humiliated; "and the entire crowd was rejoicing over all the glorious things being done by Him" (verse 17).

In other words, as Lord of the Sabbath, Jesus turned the heartless legalism of the religious leaders upside down. He shifted the debate from how much a person could get away with on the Sabbath to what kind of focus made the Sabbath truly holy. This was the point they were missing, and that's why it was an offense to them when Jesus manifested God's love and power to help hurting people for the glory of His Father on the Sabbath.

Still, Jesus did not abolish the Sabbath or minimize the importance of taking a rest from one's work. Christ had just three years to accomplish what His heavenly Father sent Him to do, yet He repeatedly withdrew from the crowds to get rest, and had His disciples do the same. He said to them, " 'Come away by yourselves to a secluded place and rest a while.' (For there were many people coming and going, and they did not even have time to eat)" (Mark 6:31).

I'm convinced that in a day when we're inundated by the demands of a wired world that never sleeps, observing a day of rest in order to focus especially on God is harder yet more desperately needed than ever. Now, you see, it's become easy, and in many cases expected, to do business 24/7/365. Packages containing oh-so-important documents for the latest deal can be delivered virtually anywhere overnight, or almost. In between deliveries, the e-mails and text messages arrive incessantly. And, of course, the phone never stops ringing (or vibrating). Consumers' insatiable appetites, the urgency of opportunities for profit, and our own works-based self-images clamor for us to paddle ever harder in the rapids of worldliness. In the midst of it all, however, Christ beckons us to be still.

"Cease striving," Scripture says, "and know that I am God; I will be exalted among the nations, I will be exalted in the earth" (Psalm 46:10). Some Bible translations begin the verse with the words, "Be still."

As the Lord Jesus underscored and restauranteur Truett Cathy understood, it pleases God for us to rest, and it's essential for our own sanity—our spiritual, mental, and emotional health—even for those involved vocationally in ministry. Regularly observing a day of rest enables us to calibrate our vision with the perspective of heaven and to focus on what really matters when measured against the standard of eternity.

And as we do so, the sound of heaven's applause can be almost audible.

DRAW NEAR AND BE TRANSFORMED

To what extent is your self-image "works-based"? In other words, do you feel like you are somehow worth less as a person if you aren't busy doing something all the time? How does God's gracious purpose for your life affect that perspective?

Is your incessant activity really driven by some kind of fear? If so, what fear? What do you have to accomplish that's more important than the work Christ had to do?

Are you more concerned with "legalistically parsing out what a person can get away with on the Sabbath than on honoring the One who established it"? How might the fact that "the Sabbath was made for man, and not man for the Sabbath" affect your view of it?

What fresh insights and blessing might God unfold to you if you made a point of regularly being still in order to know that He will indeed be exalted above all?

17

Applauded

The crowds going ahead of Him, and those who fol-lowed, were shouting, "Hosanna to the Son of David; Blessed is He who comes in the name of the Lord..."

Matthew 21:9

Jesus did not succumb to the intoxicating elixir of people's applause—He knew what was in their hearts.

The event was impromptu but the crowd grew steadily till over a million people were gawking from sidewalks, windows, and rooftops. The day was a public holiday, so that fact freed up people who would have otherwise been working to join the excited multitude. Red, white, and blue bunting adorned the streets. Eventually, a parade numbering 20,000 strong began making its way steadily along Wall Street. Spools of ticker tape began streaming from office windows and, soon, it looked like a snowstorm was filling the air. It was October of 1886, and New York City's first ever ticker-tape parade was underway.

The occasion that spawned the parade was the dedication of the Statue of Liberty. Since then, of course, dozens of heads of state, athletes, military leaders, aviators, and others have been honored with parades through the section of Manhattan that has come to be know as the Canyon of Heroes. The event for Lady Liberty, however, was the first.

Properly known as "Liberty Enlightening the World," the Statue of Liberty was given to the United States by France as a gesture of friendship commemorating America's centennial. Designed by Gustave Eiffel and sculpted by Frederic Auguste Bartholdi, the copper statue has become one of the most recognizable symbols in the world. Located in New York's harbor, it was for millions of immigrants arriving by ship their welcoming glimpse of the nation offering them freedom and opportunity. A famous inscription engraved on a plaque at the statue includes these words:

Give me your tired, your poor,

Your huddled masses yearning to breathe free,

The wretched refuse of your teeming shore.

Send these, the homeless, tempest-tost to me,

I lift my lamp beside the golden door!

During the course of His ministry, Jesus touched multitudes of "the wretched refuse" and "huddled masses yearning to breathe free" in the wreckage of fallen humanity. The tired, the poor, the homeless, and the tempest-tossed—all heard His words, saw His works, and found themselves drawn to Him.

"I am the Light of the world," He said; "he who follows Me will not walk in the darkness, but will have the Light of life" (John 8:12). "I am the door," He said; "if anyone enters through Me, he will be saved" (John 10:9).

Many have followed Him since and experienced His light and life. Person after person has realized that He alone was their hope of salvation and dared to trust Him.

When Jesus entered Jerusalem for what would be the final Passover feast of His earthly life, His arrival drew considerable attention from the curious pilgrims gathered there. Preparing for the event,

Jesus had instructed His disciples to bring Him a donkey and her colt. "This took place to fulfill what was spoken through the prophet: 'Say to the daughter of Zion, "Behold your King is coming to you, gentle, and mounted on a donkey, even on a colt, the foal of a beast of burden"'" (Matthew 21:4-5).

The disciples then "laid their coats on them; and He sat on the coats." As Jesus bounced into Jerusalem on a beast of burden, "most of the crowd spread their coats in the road, and others were cutting branches from the trees and spreading them in the road" (verses 7-8).

In other words, a spontaneous parade of the highest magnitude was underway. There hadn't been one like it before, and there's never been one like it since. "The crowds going ahead of Him, and those who followed, were shouting, 'Hosanna to the Son of David; blessed is He who comes in the name of the Lord; Hosanna in the highest!'" (verse 9).

The multitude was hailing Jesus with a greeting fit only for their coming King. The significance registered up and down the narrow streets of the crowded city. "When He had entered Jerusalem, all the city was stirred, saying, 'Who is this?' And the crowds were saying, 'This is the prophet Jesus, from Nazareth in Galilee'" (verses 10-11).

They were in fact wondering whether God's long-awaited Messiah had finally arrived. Had there been broadcast news commentators in that day, they would likely have been discussing Jesus' arrival in Jerusalem much as they now do when a contender for the American presidency comes to town. He would have been the focus of all the Sunday talk shows and His every word and move would have been subject to their scrutiny and analysis.

The days following Jesus' entry into the city held more events that brought applause from the people, though they also stirred anger and fear in His enemies. Among the first appointments on His itinerary was a visit to the temple, the same temple where, over two decades earlier, His parents found Him talking with the teachers of the Jewish law. This time, however, Jesus came to do more than just talk. His purpose was to confront the greed and corruption that enriched some while exploiting others, all in God's name.

> Jesus entered the temple and drove out all those who were buying and selling in the temple, and overturned the tables of the money changers and the seats of those who were selling doves. And He said to them, "It is written, 'My house shall be called a house of prayer'; but you are making it a robbers' den" (verses 12-13).

Further turning their established order on its head, "He looked up and saw the rich putting their gifts into the treasury. And He saw a poor widow putting in two small copper coins. And He said, 'Truly I say to you, this poor widow put in more than all of them; for they all out of their surplus put into the offering; but she out of her poverty put in all that she had to live on'" (Luke 21:1-4).

Contending with His critics directly and speaking also in parables—earthly stories with heavenly meaning—Jesus made clear that the kingdom of God consists not of humanly contrived rituals dictated by an enlightened few but in a relationship of trust and love with the Creator of the universe, and that it's accessible to "whoever believes in Him" (John 3:16). While the Jewish leaders gnashed their teeth at Him, the multitudes loved Him. Their applause, in fact, could have been a point of temptation for Jesus.

Think about it: Many people sell their soul for celebrity and worldly success—politicians, athletes, entertainers, men and women in business, and religious figures as well. History is filled with examples of individuals who got a glimpse of popularity, then chased it wherever it led—even when it meant leaving behind their integrity and morality.

The Roman philosopher Seneca, who lived during the first century, said, "You can tell the character of every man when you see how he receives praise." The Bible says, "The crucible is for silver and the furnace for gold, and each is tested by the praise accorded him" (Proverbs 27:21).

As the crowds clapped for Jesus, pleasing them rather than embracing the cross that was looming ever closer could certainly have been enticing. Jesus, however, did not succumb to the intoxicating elixir of people's applause—He knew what was in their hearts. Unlike many of the Jewish leaders, who "loved the approval of men rather than the approval of God" (John 12:43), pleasing His heavenly Father was ever Jesus' priority.

And for Jesus it would be evident all too soon that, in the words of one wit, "Having your critics praise you is like having the hangman say you've got a pretty neck."

Draw Near and Be Transformed

Imagine yourself in the crowd as Jesus entered Jerusalem. What might you have been thinking? How might you have reacted?

How do you respond to Jesus' actions and words in the temple? Do some of the same issues that He addressed still exist today? What are you doing to counter them?

Why can applause be such a test of our character? Can you think of a time when you were tempted by it to stray from God's plan for your life? How did you handle it?

"Pleasing His heavenly Father was ever Jesus' priority." To what extent would others say the same thing about you? To what extent would you say it about yourself? To what extent would God say it about you? Why?

18

Rejected

He came to His own, and those who
were His own did not receive Him.

JOHN 1:11

The Jewish leaders watching Christ from the fringes
of the crowd had no love to lose for Him. They had to
deal with Him, or life as they knew it would be over.

The menacing storm front approaching the British coast threatened to overwhelm the nation with its ruthless racism and tyranny. The storm's name was Nazism, and the sails of its leader Adolf Hitler were filled and driven by demonic winds. World War II was raging and, for proponents of freedom and democracy, things were not looking good.

Already Hitler had grabbed for territory in Austria and Czechoslovakia and intimidated other European heads of state into allowing it. When he invaded Poland on September 1, 1939, Britain and France responded by declaring war on Germany. Within four weeks, however, Poland collapsed. Even as Hitler's wicked Holocaust ovens belched their ghoulish smoke, Finland, Denmark, Norway, Belgium, Luxembourg, the Netherlands, and France also came under the heel of his brutal boot. Finally, Britain was in his sights. He was eager to drop his cold steel hammer on that nation, too.

As Hitler prepared to attack, Britain replaced its prime minister of appeasement, Neville Chamberlain, with the feisty Winston Churchill. If anyone could rally the nation against Hitler, it would be him. In his opening address to the British House of Commons on May 13, 1940, Churchill summoned his countrymen's courage with these words:

> We are in the preliminary phase of one of the greatest battles in history.... I have nothing to offer but blood, toil, tears, and sweat. We have before us an ordeal of the most grievous kind. We have before us many, many months of struggle and suffering.
>
> You ask, what is our policy? I say it is to wage war by land, sea, and air. War with all our might and with all the strength God has given us, and to wage war against a monstrous tyranny never surpassed in the dark and lamentable catalogue of human crime. That is our policy.
>
> You ask, what is our aim? I can answer in one word. It is victory. Victory at all costs—victory in spite of all terrors—victory, however long and hard the road may be, for without victory there is no survival.
>
> Let that be realized.

Christ's mission to conquer sin, death, and hell immersed Him in blood, toil, tears, and sweat...in an ordeal of the most grievous kind...in unparalleled struggle and suffering. It required Him to wage war against Satan's monstrous tyranny with all the strength His Father would give Him. Victory was His only option, and it would indeed cost Him His life—a fact that was clear as He interacted with the Jewish leaders in Jerusalem that Passover week.

The Jewish leaders watching Christ from the fringes of the crowd had no love to lose for Him. They had to deal with Him, or life as they knew it would be over. In fact, the curtain was already falling. His teachings included this parable, which cut them like razor wire:

> There was a landowner who planted a vineyard and put a wall around it and dug a wine press in it, and built a tower, and rented it out to vine-growers and went on a journey. When the harvest time approached, he sent his slaves to the vine-growers to receive his produce. The vine-growers took his slaves and beat one, and killed another, and stoned a third. Again he sent another group of slaves larger than the first; and they did the same thing to them. But afterward he sent his son to them, saying, "They will respect my son."
>
> But when the vine-growers saw the son, they said among themselves, "This is the heir; come, let us kill him and seize his inheritance." They took him, and threw him out of the vineyard and killed him. Therefore, when the owner of the vineyard comes, what will he do to those vine-growers? (Matthew 21:33-40).

The Jewish religious leaders answered, "He will bring those wretches to a wretched end, and will rent out the vineyard to other vine-growers who will pay him the proceeds at the proper seasons" (verse 41).

Jesus then responded,

> Did you never read in the Scriptures, "The stone which the builders rejected, this became the chief corner stone; this came about from the Lord, and it is marvelous in our eyes"? Therefore I say to you, the kingdom of God will be taken away from you and given to a people, producing the fruit of it (verses 42-43).

As you might imagine, the Jewish leaders didn't respond to Jesus' words with a standing ovation like that which He received from the multitude when He entered Jerusalem. "When the chief priests and the Pharisees heard His parables, they understood that He was speaking about them. When they sought to seize Him, they feared the people" (Matthew 21:45-46).

In the face of Jesus' direct affront to the positions of privilege the Jewish religious leaders had carved out for themselves, Gospel writer Mark records that they "began seeking how to destroy Him; for they were afraid of Him, for the whole crowd was astonished at His teaching" (Mark 11:18).

Reflecting later on the Jewish leaders' rejection of Jesus, Peter— the leader among the Twelve—summed it up in these words: "They stumble because they are disobedient to the word, and to this doom they were also appointed" (1 Peter 2:8).

Still, God in His love did not withdraw His gracious offer of salvation from the human race. To this very moment, it's still available to anyone who calls upon Christ: "He came to His own, and those who were His own did not receive Him. But as many as received Him, to them He gave the right to become children of God, even to those who believe in His name, who were born, not of blood nor of the will of the flesh nor of the will of man, but of God" (John 1:11-13).

Lest the Jewish leaders of Jesus' day be singularly vilified for their rejection of Him, I have to say this: Every one of us, whether Jew or Gentile, has in our own way shaken our fist in God's face. As my friend Franklin Graham has stated, it wasn't just the Jews' sin or the Romans' sin that put Christ on the cross—it was ours…yours… mine. None of us has the right to point our fingers pridefully at others as if their need for Him is greater than our own. We're all sinners guilty, in God's sight, of crimes punishable by death.

I would go on to underscore that, ultimately, Jesus' death on our behalf was His Father's plan from the very foundation of the world. Christ would die not through some unfortunate turn of circumstances, but in fulfillment of His Father's assignment.

This astounding truth causes me to exclaim with the apostle Paul,

"Thanks be to God for His indescribable gift!" (2 Corinthians 9:15). During this feast in Jerusalem, however, God's gift would be met not with gratitude, but hatred.

Draw Near and Be Transformed

The Jewish leaders rejected Jesus and wanted to destroy Him because He upended their self-centered system of values and conduct. Have you ever felt that way about Christ? When? Do you now? Why?

Can you think of a time when you looked at someone of a different race, ethnic group, economic group, or religion and thought that they were "more guilty" in God's sight than you and that you somehow deserved God's favor more than they did? To what extent were your own sins a factor in Christ's death?

Have you ever personally "received Him" and become a child of God by placing your faith in Christ for forgiveness, salvation, and eternal life? Is there anything to prevent you from doing so right now?

19

He who hates Me hates My Father also.…now they have both seen and hated Me and My Father.

JOHN 15:23-24

Finally those who hated Jesus would get the chance to show it.… In fact, it would be "open season" on the Son of God.

Hate is a strong word.

It's not necessarily a bad word but it is a strong one, and hatred is a powerful emotion.

Before you accuse me of being a hatemonger with all of its evil connotations, consider this: The English word *hate* or one of its variants, appears at least 185 times in the Bible (though references to love far outnumber it), and hate is not always mentioned in a negative sense. In fact, though "God is love" (1 John 4:8), hatred is also ascribed to Him. Examples include:

- After their exodus from Egypt the children of Israel were commanded: "You shall not set up for yourself a sacred pillar [an idol] which the LORD your God hates" (Deuteronomy 16:22).

- David declared, "The boastful shall not stand before Your eyes; You hate all who do iniquity," and "The one who loves violence His soul hates" (Psalm 5:5; 11:5).

- The Old Testament book of Proverbs asserts, "There are six things which the LORD hates, yes, seven which are an abomination to Him: Haughty eyes, a lying tongue, and hands that shed innocent blood, a heart that devises wicked plans, feet that run rapidly to evil, a false witness who utters lies, and one who spreads strife among brothers" (Proverbs 6:16-19).

- God said to wayward Israel through His prophet Isaiah, "I hate your new moon festivals and your appointed feasts, they have become a burden to Me; I am weary of bearing them" (Isaiah 1:14).

- " 'I hate divorce,' says the LORD, the God of Israel" (Malachi 2:16).

It's also noteworthy that the psalmist, speaking prophetically of Christ, said, "You have loved righteousness and hated wickedness; therefore God, Your God, has anointed You with the oil of joy above Your fellows" (Psalm 45:7).

In some situations the Bible extols hatred as a virtue to practice. Consider:

- Moses' father-in-law Jethro urged him to choose "those who hate dishonest gain" to assist him in administering the affairs of the people of Israel (Exodus 18:21).

- "Hate evil," the psalmist said, "you who love the LORD" (Psalm 97:10).

- "There is…a time to love and a time to hate," Solomon wrote (Ecclesiastes 3:18).

According to the Web site Dictionary.com, hate can be understood as a feeling of intense dislike so strong that it demands action. Viewed in this way, hatred for something evil—an intense dislike for evil that demands action in opposition to it—is good. Intense dislike for something good, on the other hand, is evil.

Confused? Think of it this way: The Bible calls us to love God and to love people, who have been made in the image of God. At the same time it calls us to hate sin, or the evil desires and actions that offend God and destroy people made in His image. So hatred, while powerful, can be either evil or good, depending on its object.

This runs counter to the thinking of our politically correct society, in which we're pressured to discard discernment and homogenize our emotions so that we either don't get too worked up about anything (that's actually apathy) or, by contrast, get equally enthused about every viewpoint and practice regardless of its merit. The byword of that creed is tolerance. God's Word cuts across this perspective, however, and demands that some things be loved and some hated.

In the case of the Jewish leaders, Jesus—the only begotten Son of God—was the object of their hatred, which made it evil. Their intense dislike for Him demanded action, and action is just what they took: "They plotted together to seize Jesus by stealth and kill Him. But they were saying, 'Not during the festival, otherwise a riot might occur among the people'" (Matthew 26:4-5).

They had an insider help them accomplish their plot.

One of the Twelve, Judas Iscariot, "went to the chief priests and said, 'What are you willing to give me to betray Him to you?' And they weighed out thirty pieces of silver to him. From then on he began looking for a good opportunity to betray Jesus" (Matthew 26:14).

That opportunity came following Jesus' last supper with the Twelve on Passover eve. During this time, Jesus not only ate with them and washed their feet; He also foretold His betrayal and death. He comforted them with promises of the Holy Spirit's presence and of His return, and He gave them instructions about prayer and relating to one another and to the world. Speaking plainly to them, Jesus made it clear that they would be hated just as He had been:

If the world hates you, you know that it has hated Me before it hated you. If you were of the world, the world would love its own; but because you are not of the world, but I chose you out of the world, because of this the world hates you. Remember the word that I said to you, "A slave is not greater than his master." If they persecuted Me, they will also persecute you; if they kept My word, they will keep yours also. But all these things they will do to you for My name's sake, because they do not know the One who sent Me. If I had not come and spoken to them, they would not have sin, but now they have no excuse for their sin. He who hates Me hates My Father also. If I had not done among them the works which no one else did, they would not have sin; but now they have both seen and hated Me and My Father as well. But they have done this to fulfill the word that is written in their Law, "They hated Me without a cause" (John 15:18-25).

No sooner had Jesus said these things to the disciples than Judas slipped out of the room to carry out his scheme. When Jesus and the rest of the Twelve departed, He headed for a spot where He frequently prayed, the garden of Gethsemane at the base of the Mount of Olives. It was on this night there, Scripture tells us, that, "being in agony He was praying very fervently; and His sweat became like drops of blood, falling down upon the ground" (Luke 22:44).

Knowing that the awful hour had come in which He would take upon Himself the sins of the world, His prayer in that moment was, "Father, if You are willing, remove this cup from Me; yet not My will, but Yours be done" (Luke 22:42).

The darkness of the shadow of loneliness that was beginning to creep over Him must have been intensified by the fact that those closest to Him—His disciples—couldn't even keep their eyes open to pray with Him. Instead, they dropped off to sleep. Judas was awake, however, and arrived right on cue, with a band of religious

Hated 137

leaders and Roman soldiers in tow in order to deliver Him into their hands.

Now, those who hated Him would—at least for a time—have their way. Finally they would get their chance to move beyond merely saying that they didn't like Him to actually showing it...and they would show it by the cruelest of means. In fact, it would be "open season" on the Son of God.

DRAW NEAR AND BE TRANSFORMED

Does it surprise you that, from a biblical perspective, hatred can be either good or evil, depending on its object, and that God Himself, who "is love," also hates some things?

Is tolerance always good? If not, why not?

What do you hate—that is, so intensely dislike that you must take action against it? Is your hatred good or evil?

How do you feel about Christ's promise to His disciples that the world would hate them just as it had hated Him? Are you willing to be numbered among those the world hates, or is it more important to you to be liked by the world?

The Bible says that "friendship with the world is hostility toward God.... Therefore whoever wishes to be a friend of the world makes himself an enemy of God" (James 4:4). What's your reaction to this statement?

20

Falsely Accused

*Now the chief priests and the whole Council
kept trying to obtain false testimony against
Jesus, so that they might put Him to death.*

Matthew 26:59

The Jewish leaders were willing to go to any length to get rid
of Him, including trumping up bogus charges against Him....
Jesus, however, entrusted Himself to His heavenly Father.

I've been in and out of prisons throughout my adult life.

My times in "the joint" began while I was still a college student. Through a mutual acquaintance, Franklin Graham and I had become friends. His mother, Ruth, had traveled to Mexico on numerous occasions and, while there, developed a burden for the hundreds of Americans then imprisoned in Mexican jails on drug charges, including not only possession of illegal drugs but also smuggling. A frequent pattern was that Americans would make trips to Mexico to purchase drugs and then bring them back to the States for sale at a quick profit.

Being a woman of action who knew that Jesus is "a friend of... sinners" (Matthew 11:19), Ruth suggested to Glenda and me that we consider spending a summer in Mexico visiting these prisoners and witnessing to them about Christ. After praying about it, we decided that this was indeed something God was calling us to do. So, with a couple of other students, we packed up and headed for Mexico. There, a gracious missionary couple took us under their wings and included us in their existing ministry to inmates.

For this well-intentioned but naïve young evangelist, the experience was an eye-opener. Just to get into the prisons, we had to pass through security screenings that sometimes included strip searches. Once we were admitted and heard the chilling sound of heavy steel doors clanging shut behind us, armed guards would escort us to visitation areas where they would then bring the prisoners.

Some whom we met were what we expected—young, callous, and belligerent. Others we encountered, however, were surprising. One young woman was pregnant when she was arrested. She had subsequently given birth and, during our visit, had her infant with her in prison. (This was especially moving to Glenda, who was pregnant with Hannah at the time.) Another inmate was actually a grandmother who had been arrested transporting drugs through the Mexico City airport!

Something that intrigued me was the number of inmates who contended that they were innocent. (As a character in one movie about prison life says, "Everybody in this place is innocent!") They told stories of being framed by corrupt officials looking for bribes— a practice that our missionary friends confirmed did sometimes take place. Whatever the circumstances of their incarceration, we talked with inmates about Christ, gave them Bibles, and offered to pray with them. After returning home, we received word from some of how God had worked in their lives—more a testimony to His faithfulness than to our skill or effectiveness!

Following our work in Mexico, I began serving as a youth pastor in a local church and, during that time, several notable instances of juvenile crime occurred in our community. Given what we had just done in Mexico, I could not help but become involved. One youth was arrested for robbing a bank and, after seeing television news footage of him gesturing obscenely at the camera when apprehended, I went to visit him in jail. He greeted me with the same attitude, contended that he was being falsely accused, and showed little interest in what I had to say.

Another youth was then arrested and charged with the gruesome murder of a neighbor. I was acquainted with his family so, again, I saw no alternative but to visit him. In contrast to the accused bank robber, this troubled teen acknowledged his responsibility and was brokenhearted and desperately hungry for the love of Christ.

Over the years, I've had opportunities to minister in numerous correctional facilities, sometimes in one-on-one conversations, other times by speaking to groups of inmates. I've visited with rehabilitated offenders about to complete their sentences and re-enter society. I've sat and talked with convicted killers awaiting their execution on death row. Along the way I've been struck by the fact that every prison is a monument to sin, and that every single inmate, whether truly guilty or falsely accused, is at the center of ripple upon ripple of tragedy and heartbreak. One prisoner sentenced to die for a high-profile murder told me, "The thing that bothers me most is the effect this will have on my grandchildren." And, of course, the victims of crime and their families never get over what's been inflicted on them. They deal with the pain, anger, and sorrow for the rest of their lives.[15]

Christ came to impart both to victims of crime and to its perpetrators forgiveness, peace, and eternal life. And all of us need what He offers because, in God's sight, all of us are guilty of sin and imprisoned by it. You can be walking around on the outside of prison and still be sin's captive. Yet, as I've seen in the lives of inmates who've come to faith in Christ, you can be locked on the inside of a prison and be free—free spiritually, free in your soul. That's the greatest need of every human being. And it was the need that Christ came to fulfill even though it meant that He Himself— the sinless Son of God—would be falsely accused.

That's exactly what happened after He was arrested. Because the Jewish leaders hated Him and felt the sting of His rebuke to their self-made righteousness, they were willing to go to any length to get rid of Him, including trumping up bogus charges against Him. Their treachery didn't come as a surprise to Jesus, however. He Himself had told the hearers of His Sermon on the Mount, "Blessed are you when people insult you and persecute you, and falsely say all kinds of evil against you because of Me" (Matthew 5:11).

"Falsely say all kinds of evil" against Him is certainly what the Jewish leaders did, but it proved to be a frustrating exercise for them:

> Now the chief priests and the whole Council kept trying to obtain false testimony against Jesus, so that they might put Him to death. They did not find any, even though many false witnesses came forward. But later on two came forward, and said, "This man stated, 'I am able to destroy the temple of God and to rebuild it in three days' " (Matthew 26:59-61).

Even then, however, Jesus did not defend Himself but entrusted Himself to His heavenly Father.

"The high priest stood up and said to Him, 'Do You not answer? What is it that these men are testifying against You?' But Jesus kept silent" (verses 62-63). Finally, they asked Him a question He did answer:

> The high priest said to Him, "I adjure You by the living God, that You tell us whether You are the Christ, the Son of God." Jesus said to him, "You have said it yourself; nevertheless I tell you, hereafter you will see the Son of Man sitting at the right hand of power, and coming on the clouds of heaven" (verses 63-64).

As you can imagine, Jesus' "yes" to that question stopped the party! At this point the Jewish leaders had heard all they needed to advance their plan to eliminate Him. They hauled Him before the Roman governor Pontius Pilate in order to use the very system of government that was oppressing them to deal with Jesus on their behalf.

> Now Jesus stood before the governor, and the governor questioned Him, saying, "Are You the King of the Jews?" And Jesus said to him, "It is as you say." And while He was being accused by the chief priests and elders, He did not answer. Then Pilate said to Him, "Do You not hear how many things they testify against You?" And He did not answer him with regard to even a single charge, so the governor was quite amazed (Matthew 27:11-14).

So amazed, in fact, that Pilate said to Him, "You do not speak to me? Do You not know that I have authority to release You, and I have authority to crucify You?" (John 19:10).

In such an hour of trial, anyone else's impulse might have been to panic or plead in order to reach some accord with his accusers. Jesus, however, said to Pilate, "You would have no authority over Me, unless it had been given you from above" (John 19:11).

Jesus knew that it was for this purpose that He had been born. Fulfilling it, however, would involve unfathomable suffering.

DRAW NEAR AND BE TRANSFORMED

Have you ever been falsely accused of something? How did it make you feel? How did you respond?

How could Christ not defend Himself, especially in view of the fate that was looming before Him?

Scripture says,

> For this finds favor, if for the sake of conscience toward God a person bears up under sorrows when suffering unjustly.... if when you do what is right and suffer for it you patiently endure it, this finds favor with God. For you have been called for this purpose, since Christ also suffered for you, leaving you an example for you to follow in His steps...while being reviled, He did not revile in return; while suffering, He uttered no threats, but kept entrusting Himself to Him who judges righteously (1 Peter 2:19-23).

If you're being falsely accused right now, take a moment to pray and ask God for His help in responding as Jesus did.

21

Suffering

*Although He was a Son, He learned
obedience from the things which He suffered.*

HEBREWS 5:8

For Him, there would be no relief.
The Son of God would die.

It loomed before us with an unequaled mix of breathtaking beauty and rock-hard resolve. As far as our eyes could see, it effused a confidence borne from thousands of years of endurance. One thing was clear: We could not master it, but it could certainly overwhelm us. Yet on this day we would venture into it—descending and, hopefully, emerging again without mishap. My two teenage sons and I were standing on the rim of the Grand Canyon.

If you've never been to the Grand Canyon, it's worth the trip. The Colorado River runs through its 277-mile length like a giant strand of liquid ribbon. A mile or more in depth at some places, the Grand Canyon's yawning breadth reaches 18 miles across at some points. Spectacular geological formations and a variety of habitats make it one of the richest natural treasures anywhere on our planet.

On this particular day, our plan was to hike from the rim to the river and back—that is, to traverse seven miles of trail that descends roughly one mile going in, followed by seven miles of trail ascending one mile coming back out.

Never mind that warning signs discouraged people from attempting to complete this trek in one day, terming it hazardous (those signs were for other people).

Never mind that a lot of people hired guides with mules to carry them in and out, and that even the mules took two days to go round-trip.

Never mind that we were getting a late start and would be hiking in the heat of the day.

Never mind (are you seeing a pattern here?) that I hadn't been exercising much lately and wasn't in the best physical condition.

We set out…and the hike down to the river actually went quite well. We made it in a little over two hours. Along the way we saw fantastic scenery and took some great photos. Once at the river, we sat and ate lunch while soaking our feet in the cool water. Then, as we packed up and started our hike back to the rim, I remember looking up and thinking, "The way out of here sure is steep and long."

About that time I also noticed the sun beating down intensely. Temperatures in the Grand Canyon can vary so extremely that you can see snow on the rim while experiencing desert heat in its depths. Before I had taken very many steps, the sun and heat were getting the best of me. My backpack grew heavier. Sips from my water bottle did not stabilize the rising temperature in my body. Profuse perspiration was soon accompanied by recurring chills. My heart rate climbed dangerously high and showed no sign of slowing. My muscles began quivering and cramping. My vision began to be distorted. My thought process became clouded. I was in trouble…in fact, I wondered if I would die. At this point the only ways out were either on foot or, all else failing, emergency helicopter airlift—how expensive and embarrassing that would be!

Gregory, who was 15 at the time and has always had the stamina of a horse, assessed my situation and accelerated his pace so that he could reach the rim and send rescuers in after me if necessary.

Nathan was just 13 but, with his innate sense of compassion, stayed with me and coaxed me along as best he could. Though Nathan carried both my pack and his own, at times I'd take just two or three steps then have to stop. Over and over again he would give me a drink and encourage me, "Come on, Dad, you're doing great. You can make it. You can do it." Nathan persevered with me step by step through the longest seven miles of my life till, with the sun setting, we finally emerged from the Grand Canyon. I was weak but we had made it. No airlift would be required. I would live to tell of this epic adventure (and *maybe* be a little more cautious).

When the Son of God came into this world, it must have been foreboding to descend from heaven into this great chasm—this Grand Canyon—filled with sin in all of its ugliness. Christ knew that the Father had sent Him to atone for the sins of the world by dying on the cross. While the cross would be the culmination of His suffering, it was not the beginning of it. From the moment Jesus was conceived, He was subject to limitations and struggles that He, as God, had never before experienced. The Bible says that "although He was a Son, he learned obedience from the things which He suffered. And having been made perfect, He became to all those who obey Him the source of eternal salvation" (Hebrews 5:8-9).

It also says, "For it was fitting for Him, for whom are all things, and through whom are all things...to perfect the author of their salvation through sufferings" (Hebrews 2:10).

How difficult it must have been for Christ to willingly forego His prerogatives as God during His time among us. I wonder whether remembrances of being with His Father before He came to earth haunted Him while He was here. If so, they did not deter Him from His mission.

The Jewish religious leaders, in their hatred of Christ as well as their jealousy for their own positions, put Jesus through their series of sham trials. Pontius Pilate, the politically correct Roman governor, became their pawn and sentenced Him to be crucified. After being betrayed by one disciple, Jesus was deserted by the rest. His closest follower, Peter, denied even knowing Him—not once, but three times.

The Bible tells us that Christ then suffered physical brutality that left "His appearance...marred more than any man" (Isaiah 52:14). (The graphic but carefully researched film *The Passion of the Christ* does the best job I know of depicting Jesus' suffering in the final hours of His life.) And Christ underwent spiritual suffering that we will never be able to fathom as, though He was sinless, He came to that hour when He would bear the sins of the world. For Him, there would be no relief. The Son of God would die.

Several years after the September 11, 2001, attacks on the World Trade Center in New York, tapes of some of the phone calls between emergency operators and those trapped in the twin towers were made public. In the moments after those demon-driven terrorists crashed jets into the buildings, as flames and poisonous gases were filling the air, you could hear operators trying as delicately as possible to help those inside understand that they were going to die.

After listening to the tapes, one news commentator said, "What an awful, awful thing to have to tell someone—that in a matter of minutes or hours they're going to die."

Well, Jesus knew that He was going to die. He saw the horror of it coming. Despite having the power to avoid it, He did not shrink from it. To the contrary, "for the joy set before Him [He] endured the cross, despising the shame" (Hebrews 12:2).

In the words of the prophet Isaiah, "As a result of the anguish of His soul, He will see it and be satisfied; by His knowledge the Righteous One, My Servant, will justify the many, as He will bear their iniquities" (Isaiah 53:11).

But as Jesus embraced the cross...oh, what anguish He would have to endure!

DRAW NEAR AND BE TRANSFORMED

Suffering willingly is a foreign concept for most of us. Yet the Son of God did just that in order to bring us to God. And no one else has done that for you or for me.

Is your attitude toward Jesus' suffering for you like that of the person who said, "Gee, I'm really sorry...but I didn't ask Him to do it"?

Or have you said, "Thank You" to Christ for what He endured on your behalf and, out of gratitude for His measureless love, dedicated your life to Him?

How do you respond to the truth that "to all those who obey Him" He is "the source of eternal salvation" (Hebrews 5:8-9)?

22

Crucified

After they had mocked Him,
they...led Him away to crucify Him.

MATTHEW 27:31

> "Your shoes hurt my feet, but
> I wore them anyway."

A man I'll call Guy had an 18-year-old son. Guy rejoiced as he watched his son grow into a teenager who was full of energy and loved the Lord Jesus Christ. What did the future hold for this promising young man?

One Sunday afternoon, Guy's son went hiking with some friends on a mountain near their home. During the hike he somehow slipped from a precipice. The injuries he sustained killed him. As a little girl later expressed it, in just a brief instant he "fell into heaven."

In the awful hours of shock and grief that followed, one visitor that came to Guy's home was a coworker named Ellis. Ellis had become a follower of Christ five years earlier and had two sons and two grandsons of his own—the younger of his grandsons was not yet four years old. Ellis felt great compassion for Guy and, as Guy later related, put his arms around their family and did what he could to comfort them. Still, though, every day for years to come, Guy would be reminded of his son's death as he drove back and forth to work and saw from the highway the very peak on which he had died.

Twenty-one years later, Ellis—by that time retired and well on in years—died. Guy attended Ellis's funeral to offer his own condolences to his family. That was a kind gesture on Guy's part...but what happened next challenged him to do more than just return sympathy.

The day after Ellis's funeral, his younger grandson—the one who was not yet four when Guy's son "fell into heaven"—also fell while rock climbing and he, too, died. Now, it was Ellis's family that was reeling in the wake of the double sorrow that had befallen them in a matter of hours. Guy faced a choice: In view of the circumstances in the death of Ellis's grandson, he could emotionally shut them out and protect himself from more pain over his own son's death. Or he could embrace their loss as his own, groan with them knowingly in prayer, and do what he could to comfort them. Guy chose the latter.

A few weeks after Ellis's funeral, in a letter to the family, Guy wrote, "I've walked a mile in your shoes. We knew exactly how you felt and what was going through your mind. In fact, your shoes hurt my feet, but I wore them anyway. We grieved with you." Guy's willingness to expose himself to pain in order to minister to Ellis's family was something they would never forget.

Jesus Christ was "a man of sorrows, and acquainted with grief." Scripture makes it clear that "He was pierced through for our transgressions, He was crushed for our iniquities; the chastening for our well-being fell upon Him, and by His scourging we are healed...the LORD has caused the iniquity of us all to fall on Him" (Isaiah 53:3,5-6). The place where all this culminated was the cross.

Crucifixion was a form of execution that the Romans sadistically perfected. A number of years ago, the *Journal of the American Medical Association* published an article cowritten by two Mayo

Clinic physicians and two United Methodist pastors, titled, "On the Physical Death of Jesus Christ."[16] In it the writers described in accurate medical detail the ghastly effects of crucifixion, with the preceding scourging, on the human body. Pain, blood loss, shock, dehydration, exhaustion, asphyxiation—these conditions and more resulted in a death that they summed up as "excruciating," which comes from a Latin term literally meaning "out of the cross." (Addressing a common misinterpretation of this event, they also concluded by saying "the assumption that Jesus did not die on the cross appear[s] to be at odds with modern medical knowledge.")

Horrible as Christ's physical death was, His greatest suffering lay in the fact that, as He hung on the cross naked with His life ebbing from Him, He was bearing the sins of the world. That, after all, was the point of His cross. That was what set it apart from all the other crosses on which the Romans executed an untold number of criminals either actual or alleged. The cross of Christ is where God ordained that sin would be addressed once and for all.

But why the cross?

The current conditions in our relationship with God are essential background for understanding the answer to this question. Only when we recognize that God is a God of love, holiness, truth, and justice, and that we through our rebellion against Him are "dead in trespasses and sins" (Ephesians 2:1 KJV) and bound for eternal punishment in a place the Bible calls hell, does the necessity of what Jesus did on the cross become apparent.

In fact, these current conditions raise what I call the Big Question: Because God is indeed a God of love, holiness, truth, and justice, and at this very moment "the wrath of God abides" (John 3:36) on us, how is it possible for us to meet with God with any outcome other than destruction?

The answer, quite simply, is that we must come to God on His terms, not ours. We must meet with God where and how He appoints. No other terms will suffice. We can only comply with or reject those terms and suffer the consequences. The meeting place of His appointment is the cross of His only begotten Son, the Lord Jesus Christ. No alternative will do—not trying to buy God's favor, not trying to earn His approval, not trying to impress Him with our achievements, not adhering to any of the world's religions. None of those measures is acceptable in God's sight. The only place where He will meet with us in order for us to be reconciled to Himself is the cross of Christ.

As Scripture says, "There is one God and one mediator between God and men, the man Christ Jesus" (1 Timothy 2:5 NIV).

Why the cross? This side of heaven none of us can fully understand this mystery. Scripture, however, does give us some helpful insights into the mind and heart of God.

First, the cross is the antidote to prideful self-indulgence, which is the essence of sin. Sin is disobeying God's law and going our own way, which results in missing the mark of His perfect standard. Christ said in Luke 9:23, "If anyone wishes to come after Me, he must deny himself, and take up his cross daily and follow Me." The cross is where our Lord Himself had to resist the taunt of His accusers, who said, "Come down from the cross and save yourself!" (Mark 15:30 NIV). The cross is the place God has appointed for us to come to Him in humble faith and obedience, in opposition to our pride, in order to be forgiven and delivered from the punishment we deserve for sin.

Second, the cross underscores our need for God and the insufficiency of our own efforts to deal with sin. In other words, we cannot fix what we have messed up.

I remember as a small boy hearing about someone who decided, for one week, to drive a nail into a piece of wood every time he did something bad. Then, the next week, every time he did a good deed he removed a nail. At the end of the second week, his good deeds had equaled his bad deeds and there were no more nails in the wood. The wood was marred, however, by the imprint of those nails. All his good deeds couldn't change that fact.

In a similar way, only God can deal with our sins. Only His Son could take "the imprint of those nails" for us. Only His Son could die on our behalf, in our place, paying the penalty for our sins so that we could be forgiven and set free. "For Christ also died for sins once for all, the just for the unjust, so that He might bring us to God" (1 Peter 3:18).

Third, the cross speaks of the necessity of shed blood for forgiveness. Leviticus 17:11 says that "the life of a creature is in the blood" (NIV). In Hebrews 9:22 we read that "without the shedding of blood there is no forgiveness" (NIV). Over and over again in Scripture we read of blood sacrifice as the way of approach to God. Indeed it was lamb's blood on the doorways of the Israelites' houses that kept them from the same fate as their Egyptian captors that first Passover. The New Testament declares Christ to be "our Passover...sacrificed for us" (1 Corinthians 5:7 NKJV).

A friend of mine once returned from traveling overseas and tried to use his leftover foreign money to pay for some items in his local grocery store. Despite his repeated attempts, the cashier would not allow it. "We do not accept that currency here," she said.

The only currency accepted by God in payment for our sins is blood—and not just any blood. It must be the innocent, pure, holy blood of His sinless, spotless Son. Nothing else will do.

Fourth, the cross is the line of demarcation between the kingdom of God and the domain of the evil one, Satan. It has become unpopular, or politically incorrect, to speak in terms of absolutes. Yet all is not relative. God and Satan, righteousness and wickedness, light and darkness, life and death, heaven and hell—each is incompatible with the other. In spiritual terms there are not shades, degrees, or increments that link them.

A ridge in the mountains near our home is marked as the Eastern Continental Divide. Water on one side of it flows to the Atlantic Ocean, while water on the other side of it flows to the Gulf of Mexico. The cross is like that: We're either on one side or the other. Paul said it this way: "May I never boast except in the cross of our

Lord Jesus Christ, through which the world has been crucified to me and I to the world" (Galatians 6:14 NIV).

Fifth, the cross is the place where God's justice is satisfied and His wrath appeased and turned away. "Once you were alienated from God," Paul wrote to the Colossians, "and were enemies in your minds because of your evil behavior. But now he has reconciled you by Christ's physical body through death on the cross to present you holy in his sight, without blemish and free from accusation" (1:21-22 NIV).

A man I know received a ticket for speeding through a small town. In that town they brought violators before the judge immediately. After this man explained as best as he could why he was exceeding the speed limit, the judge pounded his gavel and declared him guilty. Then, with a hint of kindness in his face, he said, "We run an honest court here. You've broken the law and must be fined. Nothing in the law, however, says I can't pay the fine for you. That's what I'm going to do. You're free to go."

Relieved and grateful, this man told the judge, "You've just preached the gospel!"

> He forgave us all our sins, having cancelled the written code, with its regulations, that was against us and that stood opposed to us; he took it away, nailing it to the cross (Colossians 2:13-14 NIV).

> He Himself is the propitiation for our sins; and not for ours only, but also for those of the whole world (1 John 2:2).

> God demonstrates his own love for us in this: While we were still sinners, Christ died for us (Romans 5:8 NIV).

So, the only right answer to the Big Question—the only remedy for our current condition—is the cross of the Lord Jesus Christ, for all these reasons and more. The cross is where, though our shoes hurt Him, God chose to wear them anyway. It is where, rather than shutting us out, He embraced us, grieved with us, groaned with us, tasted death for us, and made eternal comfort available to us. This mountain where His Son died, once and for all, is the one that God counts most precious, that's ever in His view, and that through time and eternity testifies to the perfect sacrifice of His Son for you and for me.[17]

DRAW NEAR AND BE TRANSFORMED

Right now say aloud, "The Son of God died for me." Go ahead... say it. If you're in a setting where it's inappropriate for you to speak loudly, say those words softly to yourself. (Don't be unnecessarily timid, though—others need this good news too!)

Say it again with this emphasis: "THE SON OF GOD died for me."

Now: "The Son of God DIED for me."

Finally: "The Son of God died for ME."

Thank God for the indescribable gift of forgiveness, salvation, and eternal life that God made available to us when Christ died on the cross.

Resolve to give the cross of Christ the place in your own life that it holds in God's heart.

23

Buried

> *I delivered to you as of first importance what I also
> received, that Christ died for our sins according to
> the Scriptures, and that He was buried...*
>
> 1 CORINTHIANS 15:3-4

Tombs defy illusion.... The One who came into this
world holy, holy, holy now lay dead, dead, dead.

As I write, my father is dying. He's been under treatment for a
serious heart condition for a number of years, but his health has
especially declined over the past few months. Now the man who
was once strong enough to carry me on his shoulders is so weak
that he must be carried. Because of strokes he has suffered, the one
who seldom lacked for words cannot now utter a single intelligible
word. The one who provided and cared for me now needs provision
and care himself.

While Daddy's death is imminent, in a real sense, all of us are
dying. The Bible says, "It is appointed for men to die once and after
this comes judgment" (Hebrews 9:27). In other words, from the
moment we're conceived and come into being, it's just a matter of
time until we leave our physical bodies.

After we die, however, we don't cease to exist. We aren't somehow recycled or reincarnated. We don't invisibly hover or float in the atmosphere. While our bodies eventually decay, our real self—spoken of in Scripture as our soul—continues on for eternity, permanently assigned by God to one of two ultimate destinations that we ourselves choose during our time on earth.

For some it's heaven, the very dwelling place of God; for others it's hell, the place prepared for the devil and his demons. Everyone goes to one place or the other, and the determining factor is whether or not, during this life, we place our faith in the Lord Jesus Christ. What we accumulate or achieve in life has no bearing on the outcome. There is only one criterion—how we respond to Christ—and there are only two options. Not to decide for Christ and His kingdom is to decide for the devil. Jesus made clear that, rather than our existence in these places being an unconscious one, we are fully aware and experience all that goes on in them forever and ever. That's why the Bible urges us over and over again to choose Christ while we can: "Behold, now is 'the acceptable time,' behold, now is 'the day of salvation' " (2 Corinthians 6:2).

Whatever our choice, those who remain behind us here after we die must deal with our bodies in some way. I've been making just such arrangements for my father, whose illness will bring his heart to a halt very soon. On my mother's behalf I've spoken with a funeral director, who will assist us by transporting Daddy's lifeless body to a facility where, according to the custom in our family, it will be prepared for burial and placed in a casket my mother has chosen. Then those who have known and loved Daddy will gather at my parents' church to grieve his departure, to reflect on what God has done in and through his life, and to celebrate the confident hope we have in Christ, whom Daddy trusted as his own personal Savior over a quarter-century ago.

Afterwards, we'll travel a short distance to a cemetery where, through tear-filled eyes, we'll watch as the casket containing his body is lowered into the ground. A granite stone bearing his name will mark the spot. There his body will remain until...well, we'll get to that. But let's not rush past this thing called burial, for after Christ died for our sins He Himself was buried and His body was placed in a new tomb that was sealed with a stone.

When someone dies, especially if it happens unexpectedly and suddenly, it is not unusual for loved ones to go through a stage of grief called denial. In other words, it can be our tendency to avoid facing the painful reality that someone dear to us has died by imagining that it really hasn't happened and that, somehow, it's all a mistake or bad dream that will go away when we wake up.

Tombs, however, defy illusion. Day after day, they are there. They state definitively that a lifeless corpse lies within and that the personality that once dwelt in that body—that once thought with its brain, peered out through its eyes, and moved with its arms and hands and legs and feet—is no longer there. Tombs assert and insist that a person is dead.

Such was the case as Jesus came one day to the town of Bethany, home to Lazarus and his sisters, Mary and Martha. A week or so earlier, Lazarus had become ill. The sisters sent for Jesus. As they waited for Him to come, Lazarus died. The sisters had no choice but to prepare his body for burial and place it in a tomb. When Jesus arrived, He was greeted by a scene of sorrow that left Him "deeply moved in spirit and...troubled" (John 11:33). In fact, upon asking the sisters where they had laid their brother, the Scripture records, "Jesus wept" (verse 35).

Think of it—the heavenly Man was moved to tears by the frailty of His earthly friends! And not just moved but, in the words of the passage, "deeply moved within" (verse 38).

On this occasion, the Lord was going to do something extraordinary. He was going to bring Lazarus back to life to demonstrate His own power and authority over death. So He ordered that the stone be removed from the entrance to the cave where Lazarus's body had been laid. When He did so, however, it's worth noting the response of Martha. She said, "Lord, by this time there will be a stench, for he has been dead four days" (verse 39).

In other words, Martha was under no illusions about her brother. She wasn't pretending that he was just snoozing. The tomb they were staring at declared indisputably that one who was once living and functioning in this world wasn't doing so anymore. Only the miraculous intervention of Christ could change that reality—and, as those present that day witnessed, He did. Jesus called Lazarus forth from the tomb and gave him yet more days here on earth. (Some suggest that the reason Jesus wept was that He had to bring Lazarus back from the heavenly bliss he was already enjoying!) Of all the miracles Jesus performed, this one especially provoked the ire of the Jewish leaders and prompted them to plot His death.

Not very long afterward, Jesus Himself would draw His last breath before a watching crowd at Calvary. After He died, Scripture records that Joseph, a Jewish leader from the town of Arimathea who had come to believe in Him, "bought a linen cloth, took Him down, wrapped Him in the linen cloth and laid Him in a tomb which had been hewn out in the rock; and he rolled a stone against the entrance of the tomb" (Mark 15:46).

As that stone came to rest, the finality of what had happened settled over Christ's followers like the dust hanging in the air. No one who witnessed His catastrophic suffering would have even considered suggesting that He had merely fainted and that, given time to rest, He would surely be back on His feet. Faced by the facts of what had taken place before them, such a thought would have been ludicrous.

Jesus had clearly died. There was no longer even the slightest pulse of life left in His body. The One who came into this world holy, holy, holy, now lay dead, dead, dead.

Draw Near and Be Transformed

Have you faced the fact that you will die, perhaps sooner than you've imagined? How do you feel about it?

Have you come to terms with the fact that, when you do, your opportunity to choose heaven rather than hell will be past?

Are you procrastinating about or trying to rationalize away your need to place your faith in Christ and be rescued from being eternally separated from God? What are you waiting for?

The stakes are ultimate and lasting. Choose Christ while you can, right now, today. If you've already done so, let the realization that eternity's clock is ticking on everyone you meet infuse you with an urgency about sharing the good news of Christ with others so that they, too, might receive His forgiveness and gracious gift of salvation.

24

Mourned

Mary was standing outside the tomb weeping...

JOHN 20:11

This grief was like sliding off the ocean's
continental shelf and sinking into an abyss.

"I'm sorry to have to tell you this over the phone," the female
voice said to me. "He is deceased."

Daddy's passing was both hard and tender.

Some 72 hours before Daddy died, as he lay in his bed laboring
to breathe, medicated for pain, and slipping from this life into eternity, Daddy had registered his last clear reaction to something I said.
Though he hadn't been moving much and his eyes were closed, when
I made a comment to him that I knew would amuse him, his mouth
broadened into a smile and he raised his arms slightly in a gesture
of happy acknowledgment. For that moment at least, he was still
engaged with those of us surrounding him.

A little later, however, he just lay there peacefully as I said to this
man God had used to bring me into being, to this man who had
modeled for me initiative, drive, responsibility, and congeniality, to
this man whose prayers, encouragement, help, and friendship had

been so instrumental in my life, to this man who later in his life had the courage to make a bold stand for Christ, "Daddy, it looks like you're going to make it to heaven before I do..." (he drew a breath).

"When you get there, you're going to be captivated by the radiance of His glory..." (another breath).

"When I get there, I want you to give me a tour..." (one more breath).

After more hours of weighty struggle and mounting exhaustion, and with my mother's loving attentiveness to his every need continuing right up until the last instant, Daddy's illness finally ran its course. He lapsed into a coma. His organs shut down. He drew his final breath. His heart stopped. He died.

In the moments that followed, before the funeral director's staff caringly wrapped his 79-year-old body for transport from my parents' home to their facility, my mother Virginia, my brother Bruce Junior, and I wept by his bed. How much we would miss him, and how different life would be without him.

At the same time, we gave thanks to God for his life and for the fact that now, because of Christ, the soul that once dwelt in this corpse was worshiping in the very presence of God. This confidence for him and this hope for ourselves as followers of Christ gave us comfort and carried us through the funeral that followed. In the printed bulletin we called it "a service of worship celebrating the presence and work of the Lord Jesus Christ in the life of Bruce Ellis Parrish, Senior," and that's just what it was. Hundreds of family members and friends who came heard not just about Daddy, but more importantly, about Daddy's Savior who offers forgiveness for sins and eternal life to all who trust Him.

Then, the day after Daddy's service, at about 9:30 in the evening eastern time, that phone call came.

"Mr. Parrish?" said a person identifying herself as a sheriff's deputy.

"Yes." Even as I spoke my mind was racing. In the course of

ministry I had served as a police chaplain for a number of years, supporting the fine men and women serving as law enforcement officers in our city. I had accompanied them to scenes of crimes and mishaps and been the bearer of tragic news to numerous next-of-kin. Whenever possible, we would communicate in person. En route to these encounters I would contemplate the fact that what I was about to say to someone would alter their lives forever. Now, it was my turn to receive such news.

The deputy explained that she was calling from the county in California where Nathan, who had graduated from college 13 months earlier, was working as a camp counselor. Because the camp was in a remote area and Nathan had been with us a couple weeks before Daddy died, we had agreed that he wouldn't make the trip back across the country for Daddy's funeral. He had already said his farewell to Daddy and would be reunited with him one day in the presence of their mutual Lord and Savior.

The deputy went on to say that Nathan had been missing for a number of hours and that their department had been called in to search for him in the rugged mountains surrounding the camp. Based on what they had learned she reported that, during some time off work, he had gone rock climbing—a sport in which I knew him to be quite accomplished and that he and Gregory had enjoyed for years, occasionally even dragging me along. She said that he had apparently been climbing on a rock face some 800 feet above its base and, with the winds blowing hard, had fallen.

Then, after pausing, she said, "I'm sorry to have to tell you this over the phone. He is deceased."

I listened quietly for a moment, the message sinking into my brain.

Nathan...deceased.

What a strange and stunning pairing of words.

What finality there was in them.

They did not allow for the possibility that he might somehow recover from the injuries he had sustained.

They did not leave any opportunity for anything else to be said or done.

They just put a punctuation mark—an unerasable, immoveable period—on the end of his life, and now those of us left behind would have to deal with it.

In that instant, our family was plunged headlong into an ocean of grief deeper than anything we were already experiencing in the wake of Daddy's passing. This grief was like sliding off the continental shelf and sinking into the abyss.

Glenda, who was sitting nearby as I took the deputy's phone call, began wailing as only a loving mother can wail, "My child, my child, my child…"

Hannah, who lived a few miles away, dissolved into tears when I told her over the phone what had happened. She and her husband, Max, rushed over to be with us.

Gregory, who after Daddy's service the day before had flown cross-country back to Seattle where he was living and working, reeled with the news that his brother—who was just 19 months younger and who had been part of his life as long as he could remember—was now gone.

JesseRuth, not yet 12 years old, was sleeping; one of the first crisis management decisions I made was not to wake her then but to tell her the next morning.

Another decision, knowing that the night was going to be long and wrenching and that the days ahead would require attention to many practical matters, was to call my friend Mel Graham, who lived nearby, and plead, "Mel, I need you here now!"

"I'll be right there," he said. *Thank God for good friends,* I thought.

Then—as Glenda sobbed in our bedroom, as Hannah and Max and also Mel and his wife, Terri, were converging on our home, as Gregory was sitting stunned in Seattle, and as JesseRuth was slumbering toward a dawn she would never forget—I found myself alone in our den at least for a few minutes.

What do you do when you're all alone and a lightning bolt has struck your world and exploded it into pieces?

I paced the room with my arms lifted to heaven, uttering from the depths of my soul a guttural prayer for help, "Oh God...oh God...oh God..." This was a time to cast myself upon the One I had followed, the One I had represented and preached all these years, and to lean hard upon His "everlasting arms" (Deuteronomy 33:27). Only He could carry us through this nightmare.

I imagine that those mourning the death of Jesus responded to that unparalleled event in all of these same ways. Some retreated to reflect. Some congregated for mutual support. Some dealt with details. Some, like Lazarus' sister Mary, just stood "outside the tomb weeping" (John 20:11). Grief is like that—it evokes from people their most basic, unvarnished instincts.

Let me quickly say that I'm not attempting here to write a treatise on grief. That's not the purpose of this book or even of this chapter. That subject is a large one and, besides, I wouldn't be qualified to do so. Others have suffered and grieved far more and, no doubt, far better than I. I'm simply making the point that Christ's death was the real death of a real person and that it brought forth real grief from people who really loved Him. And I have found that grief involves the interplay of heavenly perspective and human emotion.

Grief has been defined as pain over loss. That's the human emotion part of it. You wonder how you're ever going to be able to live with the absence of someone you love. You can't fathom that you're never going to see or hear from that person again in this life.

The heavenly perspective is this: Followers of Christ never "lose" saved loved ones because we know where they are—in heaven with Him. And one day, all who trust Him will be there as well. Going back to that truth over and over again helps you cope, in some measure, with the moment-by-moment pain.

My personal opinion, however, is that no grief is quite like grief that comes with the death of a child. This, after all, was the death

God Himself experienced. No matter how much those who've never experienced it may imagine, it is not similar to going through the death of some other loved one or friend; it isn't comparable to losing a beloved pet or anything else. It's in a class all by itself. It's a grief that must be borne…it's a sorrow that must be carried. Perhaps that's why the prophet Isaiah, in writing about the work Christ would do, said, "Surely our griefs He Himself bore, and our sorrows He carried" (Isaiah 53:4).

Grief makes you live one breath at a time…one moment at a time…one step at a time. Doing so doesn't mean that you're not experiencing the grace God promises. To the contrary, it's the grace of God that enables you to get out of bed in the morning and to do so without throwing up, or to continue functioning even when you do. It's the grace of God that enables you to handle the hard things—telling a young girl her brother has died, viewing the body of your child, picking out his burial attire, and tending to all the other arrangements that go with dealing with the remains of someone who has departed this world.

Those mourning Jesus' death waded through these waters every bit as much as we were wading through them. It was at that time that the full impact of the words spoken to Jesus' mother by the aged Simeon just days after He was born must have hit her: "Behold, this Child is appointed for the fall and rise of many in Israel, and for a sign to be opposed—and a sword will pierce even your own soul" (Luke 2:34-35).

It was also at that time that, in a way we cannot now fully understand, the Father Himself must have been mourning—even though, in the words of Isaiah, "the LORD was pleased to crush Him, putting Him to grief" so that we could be saved (Isaiah 53:10). At Nathan's funeral, his lifelong best friend Eric Chetwood—born just two weeks before Nathan—verbalized the question screaming in many people's minds when someone dear to them dies:

"Where was God when Nathan died?" Eric asked.

"I've struggled with that," he said to those in attendance, "but as I prayed about it, the answer came."

As the hundreds of people gathered in Charlotte's Central Church that day waited, Eric answered indisputably: "God," he said, "was in the same place as when His Son died."

The fact is that God's Son, the Lord Jesus Christ, not only died but was also truly mourned. His family mourned Him. His friends mourned Him. Scripture also makes it clear that, one day, even those who put Him to death will mourn Him.

Mourning for Christ, however, was not to be the last word.

DRAW NEAR AND BE TRANSFORMED

What is the deepest grief of your life? How have you responded to it?

Have you cast yourself upon the One who was "a man of sorrows, and acquainted with grief" (Isaiah 53:3), or are you still somehow trying to muddle through it on your own?

God loves you so much that He was willing to expose Himself to the pain of His only begotten Son's death so that you could receive His eternal comfort. He knows your grief. At this very moment, open your hurting heart to Him and ask Him to soothe, heal, and fill it with His sustaining, enabling grace. Pray as David prayed: "Put my tears in Your bottle" (Psalm 56:8). And thank Him that He has not left you to bear your grief alone.[18]

25

Risen

Why do you seek the living One among the dead? He is not here, but He has risen.

Luke 24:5-6

Christ's resurrection moves us beyond dead memories to living hope.

Ever notice how events with the most far-reaching implications can be expressed in the simplest of words?

Consider, for example, these headlines:

- Wall Street Crashes
- Pearl Harbor Bombed
- President Shot Dead
- Man Walks on Moon
- Berlin Wall Tumbles
- America Under Attack
- Killer Storm Approaches

Think also about these personal exchanges taking place some-where in the world at almost any given moment:

- "I love you."
- "I hate you."
- "Please marry me."
- "I do."
- "I want a divorce."
- "You're hired."
- "You're fired."
- "I'm pregnant."
- "It's a boy."
- "It's a girl."
- "It's a boy and a girl!"
- "You're innocent."
- "You're guilty."
- "You have cancer."
- "He is deceased."

Each of these concise combinations of vowels and consonants conveys occurrences that have rocked the world, or at least rocked somebody's world. Life was never the same after the events to which they refer took place.

The same is true of the resurrection of Jesus Christ. This most profound event in all of history was announced to some grieving women whose feet were wet with early morning dew in a garden outside Jerusalem with these simple words: "He has risen" (Matthew 28:6).

Simple words indeed. In fact, for persons living in a society where churches abound, those three words may even sound like a cliché or fable. But for those women then and millions of other people since, life—and eternity—has never been the same because of them. That's why it's important to hear that declaration as those first bewildered, frightened women heard it.

Think of it—their dream of salvation through the One they had believed was God's long-awaited Deliverer now lay in the cold, dark silence of death. Looping over and over again on the screens of their minds were the heartrending images of His brutal execution. They were at a loss to know what to do. So they did what grieving people often do. Before daylight had even fully arrived, they set out for His tomb.

In this case, they intended to finish the job of preparing the body of Christ for burial, something they had done only in abbreviated fashion late Friday in order to observe the fast-approaching Jewish Sabbath. Now they would add their final loving touches to the sorrowful work they had begun, even as they sought to make some sense of their shattered hopes.

To do so they would need somehow to move the stone that had been so scrupulously sealed and guarded by the Romans, upon the request of the Jewish leaders, as a deterrent to any potential claim that might surface that this Messiah had somehow beaten death and come back to life. That was the last thing the Jews or the Romans needed...but their plan was interrupted.

Early Sunday mornings often seem to have a quality all their own. The world's usual clamor is somewhat subdued. Especially in a garden, you can immerse yourself in the sights, sounds, and smells of creation that surge forth like strains from an orchestra obeying cues from an unseen Divine Conductor. Birds preen and fly and chirp. Flowers and foliage present themselves for the day with the freshness and lushness that come from the ministrations of nighttime's cool moisture, their fragrances permeating the air.

In this garden on this day, as the sky began growing light, a surprise greeted these women. Among them was Mary Magdalene, whom the Lord had set free from bondage to the dark forces of hell but who, contrary to blasphemous falsehoods currently in vogue, was never the wife or mistress of the Son of God. Scripture says it this way:

> On the first day of the week, at early dawn, they came to
> the tomb bringing the spices which they had prepared.
> And they found the stone rolled away from the tomb,
> but when they entered, they did not find the body of the
> Lord Jesus. While they were perplexed about this, behold,
> two men suddenly stood near them in dazzling clothing;
> and as the women were terrified and bowed their faces
> to the ground, the men said to them, "Why do you seek
> the living One among the dead? He is not here, but He
> has risen. Remember how He spoke to you while He
> was still in Galilee, saying that the Son of Man must be
> delivered into the hands of sinful men, and be crucified,
> and the third day rise again" (Luke 24:1-7).

I remember a time when I was traveling in a small aircraft with a friend. As the pilot, he was sitting in the left seat of the cockpit doing all the work; I was sitting in the right seat and watching the terrain pass by below. We were flying along straight and level, well into our flight of several hundred miles. The plane's single engine was droning and, as one who has spent thousands of hours in all sorts of aircraft, I was beginning to nod off into a nap. All of a sudden and literally out of the blue, an unseen force abruptly lifted us hundreds of feet, momentarily leaving our stomachs at our previous altitude. We had hit an updraft, to which my friend at the controls quickly responded, enabling us to continue on safely.

I cannot help but think that those women who came to Jesus' empty tomb that Sunday morning must have experienced something similar. They were dumbfounded. Before them was a large stone that, according to Scripture, had been moved from the entrance of the tomb by an earthquake. The Roman guards had been frightened away. Angels were speaking to the women beside a pile of vacated burial wrappings. This was not your usual graveside scene!

Far from being the end of Christ, His death and burial were now, on this morning of mornings, emerging as the prelude to an event that burst the bonds that had held creation since sin entered the world. The grave couldn't hold Him...Jesus had risen...CHRIST WAS ALIVE!

The importance of the resurrection of Jesus Christ following His crucifixion and burial cannot be overstated. If Christ did not bodily rise from the dead as He declared He would, then He was either deliberately deceptive or sadly mistaken. Such a colossal inconsistency would invalidate His teaching and undermine His credibility.

Recognizing what hangs in the balance on this point, British attorney Sir Edward Clark, once a skeptic himself, wrote, "As a lawyer I have made a prolonged study of the evidences for the resurrection of Jesus Christ. To me the evidence is conclusive, and over and over again in the High Court I have secured the verdict on evidence not nearly so compelling.... The Gospel evidence for the resurrection...I accept unreservedly as the testimony of truthful people to facts they were able to substantiate."[19]

Renowned historian Thomas Arnold declared that Christ's resurrection from the dead is the "best-attested fact in human history." And numerous other scholars have addressed the evidence for Christ's resurrection in a depth and detail that I cannot here.[20] I want to briefly highlight just a few of the implications of His resurrection for you and me.

First, Christ's resurrection announced that His sacrifice for our sins was ample and acceptable in God's sight. The apostle Paul, who had originally opposed and persecuted believers in Christ but who came to see the truth about Him, said, "If Christ has not been raised, your faith is worthless; you are still in your sins.... But now Christ has been raised from the dead" (1 Corinthians 15:17,20).

When faced with the death of a loved one, or with our own, we have no greater need than the assurance that their sins, and ours, are forgiven. Through Christ, God has made forgiveness and assurance available to anyone who will turn away from their sins and believe in Him with childlike faith. The knowledge that our son Nathan had done so has helped to make his death and absence from us more bearable. How much more ghastly it would have been to think that he was separated not only from us but also from God for all eternity!

Second, Christ's resurrection demonstrated the fact that He is indeed Lord. Preaching boldly to the throngs assembled in Jerusalem for the Jewish feast of Pentecost just weeks after Christ was crucified, the apostle Peter declared, "This Jesus God raised up again, to which we are all witnesses.... Therefore let all the house of Israel know for certain that God has made Him both Lord and Christ—this Jesus whom you crucified" (Acts 2:32,36).

In Romans 1:1,3-4, Paul wrote that he had been "set apart for the gospel of God...concerning His Son...who was declared the Son of God with power by the resurrection from the dead, according to the Spirit of holiness, Jesus Christ our Lord." Faced with issues of life and death and heaven and hell, there is no one higher or even equal on whom we can rely for our eternal well-being—not Muhammad or Buddha or Confucius, not the pope or the president or our pals. Only Jesus is Lord.

Third, Christ's resurrection marked the defeat of death, which no longer has to have the last word over us, either. The last book of the Bible opens with this declaration from Christ Himself: "Do not be afraid; I am the first and the last, and the living One; and I was dead, and behold, I am alive forevermore, and I have the keys of death and of Hades" (Revelation 1:17-18).

Peter said at Pentecost:

> Men of Israel, listen to these words: Jesus the Nazarene, a man attested to you by God with miracles and wonders and signs which God performed through Him in your midst, just as you yourselves know—this Man, delivered over by the predetermined plan and foreknowledge of God, you nailed to a cross by the hands of godless men and put Him to death. But God raised Him up again, putting an end to the agony of death, since it was impossible for Him to be held in its power (Acts 2:22-24).

Paul wrote to the Romans, "We shall also live with Him, knowing that Christ, having been raised from the dead, is never to die again; death no longer is master over Him" (Romans 6:8-9).

It's been said that we're not prepared to live until we're prepared to die. Because I have placed my faith in Christ, I have peace and a complete absence of fear as I consider the prospect of my own death. I've found that this eternal confidence enables me to face life head-on, whatever challenges it may hold.

Fourth, Christ's resurrection moves us beyond dead memories, good as they may be, to living hope. The apostle Peter emphasized this in his first New Testament letter:

> Blessed be the God and Father of our Lord Jesus Christ, who according to His great mercy has caused us to be born again to a living hope through the resurrection of Jesus Christ from the dead, to obtain an inheritance which is imperishable and undefiled and will not fade away, reserved in heaven for you (1 Peter 1:3-4).

In the weeks following that fateful call about Nathan, some well-intentioned people urged us to find solace in our memories of him. To a degree that was helpful; we do have many fond memories of his time with us, for which we are grateful. But true consolation requires more than memories. In fact, memories alone can intensify the pain of a loved one's death and haunt rather than console us. Christ's resurrection moves us beyond dead memories to living hope—hope of seeing our believing loved ones again and, more important, hope of dwelling for all eternity in the glorious presence of the Lord Jesus Christ Himself. Without this hope, memories of a departed loved one are a pitiful prelude to an eternity of unspeakable despair.

Fifth, Christ's resurrection holds the only resolution for so many of the regrets, injustices, and mysteries that are inevitable in a fallen world. If we're honest, all of us struggle with those things in one way or another. The only way we can stare them in the face and not become distracted, absorbed, or overcome by these here-and-now struggles is by looking ahead to the day when all who are Christ's followers will, in the words of Paul, "attain to the resurrection from the dead":

> Not that I have already obtained it or have already become perfect, but I press on so that I may lay hold of that for which also I was laid hold of by Christ Jesus. Brethren, I do not regard myself as having laid hold of it yet; but one thing I do: forgetting what lies behind and reaching forward to what lies ahead, I press on toward the goal for the prize of the upward call of God in Christ Jesus. Let us therefore, as many as are perfect, have this attitude (Philippians 3:11-15).

In 1884 Swiss pastor Edmund Budry wrote a triumphant hymn celebrating the resurrection of Christ. In it he declared:

> Thine be the glory, risen, conqu'ring Son;
> Endless is the victory, Thou o'er death hast won.[21]

The victory over death won by the Lord Jesus Christ offers you and me consolation, healing, freedom, power, and hope. Participating in the benefits of Christ's resurrection is not automatic, however—doing so requires a decision. The burning question that even those closest to Him had to answer following His seismic triumph is, "Do YOU believe?"

DRAW NEAR AND BE TRANSFORMED

What heart-stopping message have you received in the course of your life that, perhaps to this very moment, hangs over you like a cloud, looms before you like a wall, and stalks you like a predator? What regret, injustice, or mystery is holding you back? And what *have* you done about the fact that, in God's sight, you're like me and everyone else and need the forgiveness for sins available to us through faith in His risen Son?

Because Christ lives, tragedy doesn't have to be the last word in your life. Imagine standing on the edge of a canyon and shouting into the vast emptiness before you that thing that most pains you. Then think of the echo coming back to you—only realize that, rather than the words being the ones you uttered, they are instead different...healing...victorious:

"I've been betrayed!"...HE HAS RISEN!

"I've been violated!"...HE HAS RISEN!

"I don't understand!"...HE HAS RISEN!

"I'm dying!"...HE HAS RISEN!

"I need a Savior!"...HE HAS RISEN!

26

*See My hands and My feet, that it is
I Myself; touch Me and see…*

LUKE 24:39

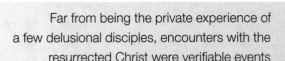

Far from being the private experience of
a few delusional disciples, encounters with the
resurrected Christ were verifiable events
that transformed cowards into lions.

Seven months before Nathan died, he ran the San Diego marathon.

At the time I did not dream that his death would soon set my own feet in motion, yet it did—and if a loved one's death can do that, how much more can Christ's resurrection cause a person to "run" with the message of His triumph?

First, the marathon. In the spring of 2005, as Nathan was serving on staff at a camp in the mountains of Southern California, he became interested in running the marathon held annually in that sparkling city by the sea, San Diego. Completing a marathon is no small task.

The modern marathon gets its name from an incident that

occurred in 490 B.C. At that time, under the rule of Darius the First, Persia attacked Greece as part of Darius's plan to dominate Europe. Some 25,000 Persian troops came ashore in the coastal city of Marathon. The Greek forces, though greatly outnumbered, successfully repelled the attack. A runner named Pheidippides was dispatched back to Athens to convey news of the victory and perhaps to warn of a possible assault on that city as well. Pheidippides ran feverishly from Marathon to Athens, delivered his message, then promptly dropped dead, probably from heatstroke.

Subsequently, his feat began to be reenacted in Athens and beyond. Today's official distance of 26.2 miles was fixed at the 1908 London Olympics, where the race was lengthened from its original distance of a little more than 24 miles so that it would finish in front of the royal family's viewing box (I'm sure the runners were delighted).

The marathon is one of the great tests of human mettle. Olympic marathon champion Emil Zatopek said, "If you want to win something, run 100 meters. If you want to experience something, run a marathon." Sports journalist Hal Higdon said, "The difference between the mile and the marathon is the difference between burning your fingers with a match and being slowly roasted over hot coals."

Well, slow roast or not, Nathan decided to run the marathon... but he committed to do so just a couple of weeks before the event. He was already in excellent physical condition, regularly running long distances in the mountains and carefully managing his diet. So, without much extra preparation, he decided to join over 20,000 other runners—many of them having trained rigorously for months—and go for the finish line. Also, as if to underscore the spontaneity of his participation (and never being very concerned with the latest fashion trends), he ran in his hiking shorts and boots, probably to the dismay of runners who had spent hundreds of dollars on high-tech running outfits.

His unorthodox attire and training regimen notwithstanding, Nathan not only finished the marathon, he finished it strongly—

better than about 90 percent of the entrants, in the top fourth of his division, and under four hours. A camera captured his image as he crossed the finish line. With his clenched fist raised, he had on his face an exhilarated look of sublime pleasure over his considerable accomplishment.

Seven months later, we featured that photo at his funeral. We captioned it with these words as a testimony to his relationship with Christ:

> Let us lay aside every weight, and the sin which so easily ensnares us, and let us run with endurance the race that is set before us, looking unto Jesus, the author and finisher of our faith (Hebrews 12:1-2 NKJV).

Many people told us what a witness it was to them.

Then, a few weeks after Nathan died, Stacey Hinnant, one of our "adopted daughters" who attended college with Hannah, began sensing that God was calling her to run the next San Diego marathon in Nathan's memory. Her plan was to ask people to sponsor her financially, with the proceeds going to a new program of the Billy Graham Evangelistic Association (BGEA) called "Dare to be a Daniel." "Dare to be a Daniel" brings adolescents face-to-face with the principles of godliness embodied in the life of the Old Testament prophet Daniel, then teaches and helps them to stand for Christ and call others to faith in Him.

Response to Stacey's idea was positive, which encouraged several others to do the same. By the time the next San Diego marathon rolled around, Team N8 (pronounced "Nate," which was Nathan's nickname) had come into being and consisted of five runners: Stacey, BGEA staffer Rob Jones and his brother Clark, our son Gregory and, gasp, me! Supporting Team N8 on site in San Diego (we needed all the help we could get since only the Jones brothers had previously done a marathon) were Glenda, JesseRuth, Hannah and Max, and another "adopted daughter," Joy Ward.

To make a 26.2-mile-long story short, Gregory took off at the starting gun and finished under four hours, with Clark and Rob not far behind. For Stacey and me, speed and time didn't matter. We ran together and tried to pace ourselves for the long, grueling distance.

Since I was the eldest Team N8 runner and hadn't seriously trained for the race beyond running my usual shorter distances, I wasn't at all sure I could do it. I thought back to my experience in the Grand Canyon and wondered if I would end up like Pheidippides. Especially through the trying miles later in the race when my energy began seriously fading, the event became a matter of mind over body. I persevered by focusing on Christ and Hebrews 12:1-2, with thoughts of Nathan, by my own passion for the kids who would benefit from "Dare to be a Daniel," and with the encouragement of our personal cheering section.

At last, Stacey and I rounded the final turn of the course and saw before us the Marine Corps Recruit Depot stadium where spectators sitting in the stands were cheering as runners crossed the finish line. I'll never forget the excitement. Nathan, who had already crossed not only this very same finish line but also now the heavenly one, came to my mind as one who was part of that great "cloud of witnesses surrounding us" (Hebrews 12:1). I imagined him looking on with amused satisfaction and saying, "Good job, Dad." I thought of my own father, who had urged me on in countless athletic events when I was a kid. At the same time I looked ahead to what I hope to experience one day when I too cross into heaven: hearing the Lord Jesus Christ say to me, "Well done, good and faithful servant." On this day, though, I'd have to settle for a finisher's medal in the San Diego marathon.

In the process of the race, we raised thousands of dollars for "Dare to be a Daniel" from generous friends—they seemed quite happy to give as long as they didn't have to run. I'm still savoring the experience. However, I do now understand about being slowly roasted over hot coals!

While Nathan's death made a marathoner out of a casual runner like me, how much more can the resurrection from the dead of the Lord Jesus Christ cause someone to "run" as a witness for Him! That's just what happened in the garden when Mary Magdalene and her companion, identified in Scripture as "the other Mary," learned that He had risen and then actually saw and talked with Him: "they left the tomb quickly with fear and great joy and ran to report it to His disciples" (Matthew 28:8).

As reports filtered back to the disciples that still more people had seen the Lord, they struggled to come to grips with what had taken place. What could it all mean? At that very moment, "He Himself stood in their midst."

> They were startled and frightened and thought that they were seeing a spirit. And He said to them, "Why are you troubled and why do doubts arise in your hearts? See My hands and My feet, that it is I Myself; touch Me and see, for a spirit does not have flesh and bones as you see that I have." And when He had said this, He showed them His hands and His feet. While they still could not believe it because of their joy and amazement, He said to them, "Have you anything here to eat?" They gave Him a piece of a broiled fish; and He took it and ate it before them (Luke 24:36-43).

Thomas, the man who has come to be stereotyped as a doubter because he was absent when the risen Christ first appeared to the disciples and insisted that he would not believe unless he could see Him for himself, actually became "the convinced one" after Christ subsequently appeared to him in the midst of the others. "My Lord and my God!" he exclaimed on that occasion. The Lord replied, "Because you have seen Me, have you believed? Blessed are they who did not see, and yet believed" (John 20:28-29).

History later ascribes to Thomas far-reaching missionary efforts, including taking the message of the resurrected Lord to India, where a group of churches bearing his name still exists today, surrounded by teeming multitudes in spiritual darkness. (Note: Despite the current hype, no second-century documents purportedly written by Thomas passed muster as being reliable Scripture.) Thomas' counterparts also pressed the gospel to the very edges of their world, even when the consequence of doing so was their own imprisonment and execution.

Luke, in introducing his Gospel account, begins by saying:

> Inasmuch as many have undertaken to compile an account of the things accomplished among us, just as they were handed down to us by those who from the beginning were eyewitnesses and servants of the word, it seemed fitting for me as well, having investigated everything carefully from the beginning, to write it out for you in consecutive order...so that you may know the exact truth about the things you have been taught (Luke 1:1-4).

In Luke's later New Testament book, the Acts of the Apostles, a sequel to his Gospel account, he writes that to the apostles Christ "presented Himself alive after His suffering, by many convincing proofs, appearing to them over a period of forty days and speaking of the things concerning the kingdom of God" (Acts 1:3).

Paul, in his summation of the gospel message, took pains to include "that He appeared to Cephas [Peter], then to the twelve. After that He appeared to more than five hundred brethren at one time, most of who remain until now...then He appeared to James [the half-brother of Jesus]" (1 Corinthians 15:5-7).

The clear challenge from both Luke and Paul was that if someone doubted the fact of Christ's resurrection, they could go to any of the hundreds of eyewitnesses who were still alive and check it out for themselves. If the resurrection had been a myth, there were plenty of people who could have said so and laid the whole matter to rest...but they didn't because they couldn't.

Within weeks of Christ's crucifixion—that dark hour when His followers fled and hid in fear for their own lives—Christ's disciples became willing to stand openly in the public square and to proclaim, without flinching, that He had risen from the dead. They would not be intimidated or silenced. They had seen Him for themselves. They had talked with Him. They had eaten with Him. They knew firsthand that His resurrection was for real.

Self-interested people do not die for what they know to be a lie. Far from being the private experience of a few delusional disciples, encounters with the resurrected Christ were verifiable events that, under the influence of the Holy Spirit, transformed cowards into lions. Jesus was really alive and they had seen Him…but they would not see Him for long.

DRAW NEAR AND BE TRANSFORMED

True biblical faith connects our minds with our hearts and sets our feet in motion. Are you allowing the resurrection of Christ to move you toward others with the astounding news of His triumph?

If not, what hesitations and fears do you need to face and deal with in order to be a courageous witness for Him?

In what surprising ways might God want to use you for His glory? Will you allow the Holy Spirit to empower you to do His will?

27

Ascended

*After He had said these things, He was
lifted up while they were looking on, and a
cloud received Him out of their sight.*

ACT 1:9

His "awayness" does not constitute
our aloneness.

Are you afraid to be alone?

Or, more to the point, does being alone make you feel sad and
envelop you in that aching condition called loneliness?

For many people this is the case, and they'll go to great lengths
to avoid it—or at least to minimize the experience. They'll sit in
restaurants or bars among individuals they don't even know, just
to be in the presence of others (even then they can still be lonely).
They'll switch on a television set in their home just to have a background of human noise even though the shows and commercials
don't really interest them. They'll spend hours at a time surfing the
Internet, sending instant message after instant message, chatting,
posting, and blogging, all in order not to feel quite so alone.

Such measures can, in reality, be an attempt to avoid having to deal with personal issues, including one's need for Christ. Charles Caleb Colton wrote in the early 1800s, "To dare to live alone is the rarest courage; since there are many who had rather meet their bitterest enemy in the field, than their own hearts in their closet." Frequently it's in solitude that we come face to face with the dark emptiness in our hearts and lives that only the Lord Jesus Christ can light and fill.

In the course of my life and ministry I've spent a great deal of time not only being among many people but also being alone. More often than not in my travels to speaking engagements and other activities, circumstances have necessitated me going solo rather than in a larger party. In distant cities, after being with small groups and large audiences, I've returned time and time again to a hotel room alone.

Don't misunderstand—I'm not complaining. For the most part I enjoy and even thrive on being able to read, pray, reflect, write, work, and relax away from clamor. It's not unusual for me to spend several days operating out of a hotel room without ever turning on the television, except perhaps to catch up on the news. Nor do I spend long stretches on the Internet. I just don't need such distractions; some of my most energizing, transforming moments of insight come when I'm by myself. Still, though, even I sometimes have to press on through aching loneliness, especially for Glenda and our children.

The late secretary-general of the United Nations Dag Hammarskjold once said, "Pray that your loneliness may spur you into finding something to live for, great enough to die for." I'm grateful to say that, in Christ, this has been my experience. For Christ's first followers too, what happened after His resurrection appearances moved them both to live and to die for Him.

Luke tells us that, after "a period of forty days," Christ gathered His disciples and "commanded them not to leave Jerusalem, but to wait for what the Father had promised, 'Which,' He said, 'you heard of from Me; for John baptized with water, but you will be baptized with the Holy Spirit not many days from now'" (Acts 1:4-5).

He went on to explain: "You will receive power when the Holy Spirit has come upon you; and you shall be My witnesses both in Jerusalem, and in all Judea and Samaria, and even to the remotest part of the earth" (Acts 1:8). Empowered by the Holy Spirit, this ragtag band of ordinary men would in fact come to be known as those who "turned the world upside down" (Acts 17:6 KJV). Through them the church—the fellowship of Christ's followers also referred to in Scripture as Christ's "body" (see Ephesians 5:23)—would grow into a worldwide force for His kingdom.

Then, Luke reports, "after He had said these things, He was lifted up while they were looking on, and a cloud received Him out of their sight" (Acts 1:9).

In his Gospel account, Luke provides additional details. There he says, "He led them out as far as Bethany, and He lifted up His hands and blessed them. While He was blessing them, He parted from them and was carried up into heaven" (Luke 24:50-51).

In my own imagination I picture what the disciples witnessed that day as being somewhat akin to watching the quiet but sure ascent of a person in a hot air balloon—only without the balloon! However it happened, according to Scripture, it left them standing there with their necks craned and straining to see the One who had just been right there before them but who had now disappeared into a cloud.

At that moment, these ordinary people who had shared intimately for three years in the earthly life of the Son of God...who had listened as He spoke and watched as He performed unprecedented miracles...who had seen crowds throng to Him and then turn against Him...who had watched Him be beaten and battered, then crucified...who had struggled to pick up the pieces of their lives when their Master was dead, only to find out that He had risen...these people now faced a new dimension in their relationship with Him.

They had to deal with His "awayness"—the fact that, while He was not in a place where they could see and touch Him physically,

He was very much alive and had charged them with the responsibility of representing Him and carrying on His work. Thankfully, on this occasion as well as previously, Christ promised them that the Holy Spirit would be with them and, in fact, *in* them to empower and enable them to fulfill this mission. He was referring to the experience they would have soon afterward on the Jewish Day of Pentecost, which marked the beginning of the early church's explosive growth, as well as to the ongoing experience of believers today.

He told them even before He was crucified:

> I will ask the Father, and He will give you another Helper, that He may be with you forever; that is the Spirit of truth, whom the world cannot receive, because it does not see Him or know Him, but you know Him because He abides with you and will be in you…. the Helper, the Holy Spirit, whom the Father will send in My name, He will teach you all things, and bring to your remembrance all that I said to you….

> When the Helper comes, whom I will send to you from the Father, that is the Spirit of truth who proceeds from the Father, He will testify about Me, and you will testify also, because you have been with Me from the beginning….

> But I tell you the truth, it is to your advantage that I go away; for if I do not go away, the Helper will not come to you; but if I go, I will send Him to you. And He, when He comes, will convict the world concerning sin and righteousness and judgment; concerning sin, because they do not believe in Me; and concerning righteousness, because I go to the Father and you no longer see Me; and concerning judgment, because the ruler of this world has been judged….

> But when He, the Spirit of truth, comes, He will guide you into all the truth; for He will not speak on His own

initiative, but whatever He hears, He will speak; and He
will disclose to you what is to come. He will glorify Me,
for He will take of Mine and will disclose it to you (John
14:16-17,26; 15:26-27; 16:7-14).

Christ's promise of the Holy Spirit's presence in the lives of His
followers after His ascension represented, to use a term of today, a
paradigm shift of the highest order. In His physical absence they
would have not just memories of their time with Him here and
anticipation of being with Him again eventually in heaven, but
they would have His very presence always with and in them. In
other words, His "awayness" would not constitute their aloneness,
nor does it for us. That's a very different experience than we have
following the departure of even our saved loved ones.

Nathan and Daddy are no longer physically present in this world.
I cherish the memories of their time with me here, and I have great
anticipation of being with them in heaven. The fact is, however,
they are away…they are absent…they are not with me here now in
any form either physical or spiritual. Despite what I may desire or
imagine, I cannot communicate with them. At this very moment,
however, Christ is very much present in the lives of all who love
Him, not just figuratively but literally, through the person of the
Holy Spirit. We can still commune with Him step by step, day by
day in all the circumstances of life.

Knowing that His followers needed reassurance in facing the
task before them while He was away, Christ said to them, "Peace I
leave with you; My peace I give to you; not as the world gives do I
give to you. Do not let your heart be troubled, nor let it be fearful"
(John 14:27).

Matthew records that, before He ascended,

Jesus came up and spoke to them, saying, "All authority
has been given to Me in heaven and on earth. Go therefore and make disciples of all the nations, baptizing them
in the name of the Father and the Son and the Holy

Spirit, teaching them to observe all that I commanded you; and lo, I am with you always, even to the end of the age" (Matthew 28:18-20).

It was then, Scripture tells us, that "when the Lord Jesus had spoken to them, He was received up into heaven and sat down at the right hand of God" (Mark 16:19). In the words of the writer of the New Testament letter to the Hebrews, "When He had made purification of sins, He sat down at the right hand of the Majesty on high" (Hebrews 1:3).

The privilege and status of being seated "at the right hand of the Majesty on high" belongs only to the risen, ascended Son of God. He alone

> was revealed in the flesh,
> was vindicated in the Spirit,
> seen by angels,
> proclaimed among the nations,
> believed on in the world,
> taken up in glory (1 Timothy 3:16).

However, Christ's ascension by no means marked the end of His involvement in earthly matters.

DRAW NEAR AND BE TRANSFORMED

Do you seek to avoid being alone so that you won't have to face issues and needs in your life, including your need for Christ? In what ways?

How might Christ's promise to be present with and in the lives of His followers by the Holy Spirit change the way you view and deal with your responsibilities and pressures?

Have you ever been conscious that the Holy Spirit was teaching you about Christ and using you as a witness for Him? In what situations?

Do you see the difference between having a dynamic relationship with Christ presently as compared with having just memories of, and anticipation of reunion with, your loved ones who have already gone to heaven?

Part Three:

Since He Departed

Holy, holy, holy is the Lord God, the Almighty,
who was and who is and who is to come.

REVELATION 4:8

28

Interceding

He is able also to save forever those who draw near to God through Him, since He always lives to make intercession for them.

After Christ finished His work of redemption, rose from the grave, and ascended to His Father, He embraced His unfinished work—namely, being the ongoing intermediary between God and people.

Children are masters at figuring out how to get what they want. After they've gained enough experience to realize that the direct approach ("Can I have…?") doesn't always work ("No"), they begin developing other strategies for fulfilling their desires.

Without being able to articulate it, even a preschooler intuitively understands that it's sometimes better to approach the decision-making parent through an intermediary—maybe the other parent, an older brother or sister, or a favorite aunt or uncle or grandparent—one who possesses certain essential attributes.

To be effective, this intermediary has to be aware of and sympathetic toward the child's "need." This intermediary is also required to have credibility in the eyes of the decision-making parent. He or she also needs access to that parent, an opportunity to state the child's case. And finally, the intermediary must find favor with the parent in the particular situation at hand so that the request will be granted.

A well-executed plan is a beauty to behold. In our family, for example, just such a strategy was employed by our daughter Jesse-Ruth in obtaining a certain desire of her heart—namely, a dog. And not just any kind of dog, mind you, but a dog that could live *inside* our home!

We had owned dogs before, as Hannah, Gregory, and Nathan were growing up. The first one—an adorable mixed-breed we purchased at the pound—savagely bit the delivery man, so his time with us was short-lived. Next we had a registered golden retriever that came to us when she was about a year old, apparently because she had presented her original owners with some behavior problems. Before we could have her spayed she promptly ran off with a chow chow and produced one of the ugliest mongrel puppies I've ever seen—one that, in fact, was incontinent and perpetually wet on people's feet. Neither of these dogs, however, gained admission to the inner sanctum of our home (not while I was around anyway). They stayed in the garage or in a doghouse in the backyard. Eventually, each one took its leave and we were once again (whew!) dogless. Then JesseRuth started wanting one.

The wheedling that followed was shameless. In my resistance to the idea I came off as the hard-hearted bad guy—a sort of real-life Cruella De Vil of the male variety. JesseRuth, who was about seven at the time, then utilized Glenda as her intermediary. Glenda, after all, had all the right attributes—she was sympathetic, she had credibility with and access to me, and she had ways of being quite influential. Finally, I caved in. For JesseRuth's eighth birthday we drove a hundred miles or so to pick up just the right dog for her—one from a breed that I was embarrassed even to mention to my manly friends—one that was called a Yorkie Poo. You can imagine how conversations went as, while walking this little ball of fur around the neighborhood, we encountered other dog owners.

"Hi…nice day…that's a fine looking German shepherd you have there."

"Thanks…and what kind of dog is that?"

"A Yor(mumble)."

"A what?"

"A (cough)oo."

"Say again?"

"All right…a YORKIE POO."

"Hey…no problem…to each his own."

As we resumed walking, I'd then look down to where our Yorkie Poo had just been sitting—on my foot—and see a pronounced wet spot!

Nonetheless, with time I've adjusted. JesseRuth named her dog Sercy—which means "surprise"—and much to my surprise, I actually enjoy having Sercy around. Still, though, she wouldn't be living with us if Glenda had not acted as an intermediary on JesseRuth's behalf.

After Christ finished His work of redemption, rose from the grave, and ascended to His Father, He embraced what I think of as His unfinished work—namely, being the ongoing intermediary between God and people. As the New Testament writer to the Hebrews said, "He is able also to save forever those who draw near to God through Him, since He always lives to make intercession for them" (Hebrews 7:25).

In other words, at this very moment Christ is representing to His Father the needs and desires of all who trust Him, and He does so continuously. He is uniquely qualified to do so because He is aware of and sympathetic toward our needs, has unequaled credibility with the Father, and has uninterrupted access to Him. And when He states our case, He always receives a favorable hearing.

"For it was fitting for us to have such a high priest," Hebrews goes on to say, "holy, innocent, undefiled, separated from sinners and exalted above the heavens; who does not need daily…to offer up sacrifices, first for His own sins and then for the sins of the people, because this He did once for all when He offered up Himself" (Hebrews 7:26-27).

As the hymn writer of old declared, "What a Friend we have in Jesus"!

It's also important for us to realize that, at the same time Jesus is interceding for us, the Holy Spirit, who dwells in all who have trusted Christ, is doing so as well. The apostle Paul wrote:

> In the same way the Spirit also helps our weakness; for we do not know how to pray as we should, but the Spirit Himself intercedes for us with groanings too deep for words; and He who searches the hearts knows what the mind of the Spirit is, because He intercedes for the saints according to the will of God (Romans 8:26-27).

The picture that emerges, then, is this: Since Christ departed, He has been engaged in personally representing the needs of His followers in the very presence of His Father. Simultaneously, the Holy Spirit—who also perfectly understands the will of the Father—is at work helping Christ's followers in prayer. And as Christ's followers, we are instructed to "pray at all times" (Ephesians 6:18). Jesus told the disciples that "if you ask the Father for anything in My name, He will give it to you…. for the Father Himself loves you, because you have loved Me and have believed that I came forth from the Father" (John 16:23,27).

What all this means is that, though Christ is not now physically present on earth, a dynamic relationship of loving communion exists between the Father, the Son, and the Spirit, and all those who have become children of God through faith in Christ. This wondrous truth caused Paul to exclaim:

> He who did not spare His own Son, but delivered Him over for us all, how will He not also with Him freely give

us all things? Who will bring a charge against God's elect? God is the one who justifies; who is the one who condemns? Christ Jesus is He who died, yes, rather who was raised, who is at the right hand of God, who also intercedes for us. Who will separate us from the love of Christ? Will tribulation, or distress, or persecution, or famine, or nakedness, or peril, or sword?...in all these things we overwhelmingly conquer through Him who loved us (Romans 8:32-35,37).

And in case this thrilling reality isn't enough, guess where this communion and love are heading—straight toward "the next big thing": Christ's glorious return to earth.

DRAW NEAR AND BE TRANSFORMED

To what extent do you live with the awareness that Christ is interceding with His Father for you? What difference does it make?

According to Scripture Christ is uniquely qualified for this work, yet many people look to other intermediaries in a desperate attempt to find favor with God. Why is this futile, and even an insult to Christ?

Have you ever sensed the Holy Spirit assisting you in prayer? When?

To what extent would you define your experience of prayer as participation in ongoing, dynamic communion with the Father, the Son, and the Holy Spirit?

Pause right now to thank God that, whatever life may hold, you can "overwhelmingly conquer" through Him who loves you.

29

Returning

*This Jesus, who has been taken up from
you into heaven, will come in just the same way
as you have watched Him go into heaven.*

Acts 1:11

The return of Christ that's promised is not just a
figurative one—it is a literal event still to occur,
just as surely as He literally came the first time.

The waiting seemed to go on forever.

In fact, it lasted 31.5 seconds. During that time, however, no one knew whether those who had traveled so far and endured so much would actually be successful in returning safely to earth. I'm referring to the crew of Apollo 13.

The third American manned lunar landing mission was launched from Cape Canaveral in Florida on April 11, 1970. Two days later, with the crew of James Lovell, John Swigert, and Fred Haise 200,000 miles from earth, one of the oxygen tanks in their spacecraft exploded, resulting in a loss of not only oxygen but also electrical power. Over the radio in Mission Control in Texas crackled the now-famous words from Commander Lovell: "Houston, we've had a problem."

Scrapping plans for a lunar landing, NASA's revised sole objective for the mission became the safe return of the astronauts. No one knew whether this could be achieved. Attempting their return required that the astronauts transfer themselves from their damaged main craft to the lunar landing module they had in tow. Mission controllers also had to figure out how to sustain three people for four days in a craft that had been designed to support only two people for two days. The crew also had to be able to navigate in space, survive a fiery reentry to earth's atmosphere, and splash down in the ocean. The challenges were so great that some observers put the odds for their safe return at no higher than one chance out of ten.

The crew's fate, however, wasn't left to chance. While some of the brightest minds in the world focused on overcoming the technical problems, the Congress of the United States called on Americans to pray. And that's just what happened: In homes, offices, and churches not only in the United States but in other places as well, people prayed fervently.

Finally, after nearly six full days in space that included a quick pass around the far side of the moon, which helped to "slingshot" the crew back toward earth, the moment of reentry into our atmosphere came. This superheated stage of space travel always involves a period of radio blackout, but experts say that its duration is predictable down to the second. After Apollo 13 entered radio blackout and enough time had elapsed for communication to resume, however, the radios remained silent. As seconds ticked by on the clock, the questions loomed in the air:

Had something gone wrong on reentry?

Had the craft drifted off course?

Had the jury-rigged equipment failed?

Would the crew return after all?

Then, 31.5 seconds late—a delay still not fully explained—the radio came alive:

"Houston, this is Apollo 13..."

Elated staffers and family members cheered and hugged as the happy outcome that had seemed so unlikely did indeed come to pass. That moment of jubilation pales, however, in comparison with what will take place when the Lord Jesus Christ returns to earth.

While waiting for Christ's return to earth seems to go on forever and at times appears unlikely, this next big event in the history of the world will indeed come to pass, just as the Bible declares. And the return of Christ that's promised is not just a figurative one—it is a literal event still to occur, just as surely as He literally came the first time. As Jesus ascended from the Mount of Olives, His disciples were greeted by two angels who assured them of this fact:

> As they were gazing intently into the sky while He was going, behold, two men in white clothing stood beside them. They also said, "Men of Galilee, why do you stand looking into the sky? This Jesus, who has been taken up from you into heaven, will come in just the same way as you have watched Him go into heaven" (Acts 1:10-11).

Jesus Himself said to His disciples, "In My Father's house are many dwelling places; if it were not so, I would have told you; for I go to prepare a place for you. If I go and prepare a place for you, I will come again and receive you to Myself, that where I am, there you may be also" (John 14:1-3).

Of course, skeptics of Christ's return abound. They point to the millennia that have now elapsed since He first came, as well as multiple false prophecies through the centuries about specific dates for His return (something Christ said that no one knows except the Father), and they dismiss the idea as a fabrication of delusional zealots. In essence, however, they themselves are predicting the future—they are saying that Christ *won't* return—based upon the "seconds" ticking by during this current period of "blackout." Over and over again, the Bible—the same Book that foretold with accuracy Jesus' first coming—warns against doing so.

> Know this first of all, that in the last days mockers will
> come with their mocking, following after their own lusts,
> and saying, "Where is the promise of His coming? For
> ever since the fathers fell asleep, all continues just as
> it was from the beginning of creation."... But do not
> let this one fact escape your notice, beloved, that with
> the Lord one day is like a thousand years, and a thou-
> sand years like one day. The Lord is not slow about His
> promise, as some count slowness, but is patient toward
> you, not wishing for any to perish but for all to come
> to repentance. But the day of the Lord will come like a
> thief...(2 Peter 3:3-4,8-10).

Scripture makes it clear that when Christ comes again, it will
not be as a baby in a manger. He will do so with power and glory
to put down the raging forces of wickedness and to establish His
righteous kingdom. Understanding of the prophesied sequence of
events varies.[22] My conviction from my study of Scripture is that
Christ's return will be preceded by the resurrection of those who
have died believing in Christ—including Daddy and Nathan—as
well as the rapture, or instantaneous evacuation, of the followers of
Christ living at that time. As the apostle Paul wrote:

> The Lord Himself will descend from heaven with a shout,
> with the voice of the archangel and with the trumpet of
> God, and the dead in Christ will rise first. Then we who
> are alive and remain will be caught up together with them
> in the clouds to meet the Lord in the air, and so we shall
> always be with the Lord (1 Thessalonians 4:16-17).

With the world groaning through a period of unprecedented tribulation in the grip of the blasphemous Antichrist—who will be bent
on carrying out Satan's ancient schemes of deceit and destruction—
Christ will once again set foot on the Mount of Olives, leading the
redeemed in a victorious train of triumph and vanquishing His
warring foes. This will be the day that Job of old anticipated when

he, by faith, declared: "As for me, I know that my Redeemer lives, and at the last He will take His stand on the earth. Even after my skin is destroyed, yet from my flesh I shall see God; whom I myself shall behold, and whom my eyes will see and not another" (Job 19:25-27).

We live in a day when news broadcasts regularly report on upheavals of potentially cataclysmic proportion in the Middle East. Consider also that, over the past 100 years, two world wars have been fought, the creation and proliferation of nuclear weapons has occurred, the modern state of Israel was born, the capacity to communicate instantaneously and globally has become commonplace, and computerized world banking systems have been established. At the same time, the gospel of Christ is being proclaimed across the globe via satellite and radio as well as by missionaries, churches, and Christian organizations. Viewed in the light of biblical prophecy, these developments are not incidental. Christ's return and the events surrounding it—described in Scripture in considerable detail—could unfold at any moment. This calls for attention, study, and preparation so that we are not caught unaware.

For the enemies of Christ, His return will be a time of unimaginable sorrow; for His followers, it will be a time of rejoicing. Because eternity in either heaven or hell hinges upon how we respond to Christ, now is the time to make sure we're ready for His return—whether it occurs before we go to our grave or as we're coming out of it!

> For yet in a very little while, He who is coming will come,
> and will not delay (Hebrews 10:37).

And once He's here again, the world will witness a reign like it's never seen before.

Draw Near and Be Transformed

Do you believe in the literal return to earth of Christ? Why or why not? What bearing does God's perspective of time have on your belief?

Based upon what you know about events surrounding the return of Christ, what are your thoughts about the significance of recent world developments?

If Christ were to return at this very moment, what would your first thought be? What have you left unsaid or undone that you would regret? Do whatever you can about it right now.

30

Ruling

*The kingdom of the world has become
the kingdom of our Lord and of His Christ;
and He will reign forever and ever.*

REVELATION 11:15

In that coming day, and even now, those
who want to please Him will lovingly speak His
name, act in His name, and live for His name.

I have a confession to make.

I'm glad I'm not the man who came to be known as His Royal Highness the Prince Charles Philip Arthur George, Prince of Wales, Duke of Cornwall and Earl of Chester, Duke of Rothesay, Earl of Carrick, Baron of Renfrew, Lord of the Isles, Prince and Great Steward of Scotland, Knight Companion of the Most Noble Order of the Garter, Knight of the Most Ancient and Most Noble Order of the Thistle, Great Master and First and Principal Knight Grand Cross of the Most Honourable Order of the Bath, Member of the Order of Merit, Knight of the Order of Australia, Companion of the Queen's Service Order, Member of Her Majesty's Most Honourable Privy Council, Aide-de-Camp to Her Majesty—or, for short, Prince Charles.

From birth, almost every move of Britain's heir to the throne was scrutinized, reported, analyzed, second-guessed, and gossiped about—and yet, after roughly six decades, the man didn't spend a single day as king! Rather than establishing a legacy based on reigning, he became better known perhaps as the one whose marriage to Her Royal Highness the Princess Charles, Princess of Wales and Countess of Chester, Duchess of Cornwall, Duchess of Rothesay, Countess of Carrick, Baroness of Renfrew, Lady of the Isles, Princess of Scotland—or, for short, Princess Diana—ended in divorce and who later married his acknowledged mistress Camilla Parker Bowles.

His is a strange tale—especially in comparison to that of the King of kings and Lord of lords, Jesus Christ. Christ never spent one day "in waiting"—He was born King. When He appeared, wise men from the East arrived in Jerusalem, saying, "Where is He who has been born King of the Jews? For we saw His star in the east and have come to worship Him" (Matthew 2:2). While Jesus is certainly the "Prince of Peace" (Isaiah 9:6), He is also King, but not after the order of this world. He declared to Pontius Pilate, "My kingdom is not of this world" (John 18:36).

In fact, Scripture makes clear that when Christ returns to earth, the kingdom He establishes here will transform this world into something far different than it is now—a place of righteousness, peace, justice, prosperity, and pervasive kindness. Satan will be "bound...for a thousand years" (Revelation 20:2). Those who have followed Christ—referred to in Scripture as Christ's "bride"[23]—will reign with Him.

Of this time the Bible says, "The LORD will be king over all the earth; in that day the LORD will be the only one, and His name the only one" (Zechariah 14:9). In other words, the fact that history and life really are all about Him will finally be fully evident. His name and His name alone will be the only one that matters.

After Nathan died and we began our emotional journey of coming to terms with his absence, we learned about a missionary couple in Africa whose son had also died. Upon hearing their deceased son's name mentioned by a friend, they began to weep. Concerned that she might have offended the grieving parents, the friend quickly apologized. The parents, however, responded by saying, "We are weeping for joy. No one else will say his name to us for fear of upsetting us. It was just so good to hear his name again."

God loves to hear the name of His only begotten Son, the Lord Jesus Christ, who died on Calvary's cross for the sins of the world. In that coming day, and even now, those who want to please Him will lovingly speak His name, act in His name, and live for His name.[24]

After Satan has been bound for 1000 years, he will be released to incite one last uprising against Christ (see Revelation 20:7-9). However, at that point, the world as we know it will be consumed with fire. As Peter wrote:

> By His word the present heavens and earth are being reserved for fire, kept for the day of judgment and destruction of ungodly men.... the heavens will pass away with a roar and the elements will be destroyed with intense heat, and the earth and its works will be burned up (2 Peter 3:7,10).

The Bible says that the devil and his demons will be "thrown into the lake of fire and brimstone...and they will be tormented day and night forever and ever" (Revelation 20:10). What's referred to in Scripture as the "great white throne" judgment will also take place (verse 11). There, "the dead, the great and the small" will be "judged from the things...written in the books, according to their deeds" (Revelation 20:12). In that awful moment, anyone whose name is "not found written in the book of life"—as a result of trusting in Christ—will be thrown into "the lake of fire" (Revelation 20:15).

> Then comes the end, when He hands over the kingdom to the God and Father, when He has abolished all rule and all authority and power. For He must reign until He

has put all His enemies under His feet. The last enemy
that will be abolished is death.... When all things are
subjected to Him, then the Son Himself also will be subjected to the One who subjected all things to Him, so
that God may be all in all (1 Corinthians 15:24-26,28).

While these events may sound disconcerting, those who have
trusted in Christ for forgiveness, salvation, and eternal life have no
reason to fear. All who have personally experienced that it is "by
grace you have been saved through faith; and that not of yourselves,
it is the gift of God; not as a result of works, so that no one may
boast" (Ephesians 2:8-9) will dwell safely, securely, and forever, in
a new heaven and new earth that has a new Jerusalem as its center-
piece. Scripture describes that coming age this way:

Behold, the tabernacle of God is among men, and He
will dwell among them, and they shall be His people,
and God Himself will be among them, and He will wipe
away every tear from their eyes; and there will no longer
be any death; there will no longer be any mourning, or
crying, or pain; the first things have passed away (Revelation 21:3-4).

Scripture goes on to say that "the city has no need of the sun or of
the moon to shine on it, for the glory of God has illumined it, and its
lamp is the Lamb. The nations will walk by its light, and the kings
of the earth will bring their glory into it" (Revelation 21:23-23).

Much to the chagrin of some, the official motto of the United
States of America since 1956 has been "In God We Trust." (A varia-
tion of the phrase was actually penned by Francis Scott Key, author
of America's national anthem, "The Star-Spangled Banner," during
the War of 1812.) To commemorate the fiftieth anniversary of the
motto in July 2006, President George W. Bush issued an official
proclamation in which he spoke of "a divine plan that stands above
all human plans."

The divine plan that stands above all human plans is, quite simply, the exaltation of God's Son. As the apostle Paul wrote,

> For this reason also, God highly exalted Him, and bestowed on Him the name which is above every name, so that at the name of Jesus every knee will bow, of those who are in heaven and on earth and under the earth, and that every tongue will confess that Jesus Christ is Lord, to the glory of God the Father (Philippians 2:9-11).

As for me, I'm already bowing my knees in worship...and I'm looking forward to doing so for all eternity.

Draw Near and Be Transformed

In what ways do you think Christ's kingdom is different from the kingdoms of this world?

How frequently, and in what ways, do you speak the name of Jesus Christ?

Does the prospect of the great white throne judgment frighten you? Does it give you any sense of responsibility or urgency for others' well-being?

To what extent does your view of the future extend beyond your own physical death? What place do you see yourself having in the coming events described in Scripture?

31

Worshiped

*Worthy is the Lamb that was slain to
receive power and riches and wisdom and
might and honor and glory and blessing.*

REVELATION 5:12

Worship is the agenda of heaven.

Last night I saw a vast multitude assembled for one great purpose.
Among the throng were people of many ethnic backgrounds. In the
crowd I heard snippets of languages from across the world. I myself
found a place to stand just yards away from the towering structure
that was the focus of every eye for miles. Its striking mass dwarfed
me. The elevated plateau on which it stood gave me—as well as
Glenda and JesseRuth, who were with me—a vantage point from
which to survey the sea of people surrounding it. In the distance
we could see a river. We could also see to the north, east, south,
and west memorials that were bathed in unwavering light and that
brought to mind individuals who had preceded us and to whom we
owed so much. Also in view were edifices housing their legacy. As
music filled the air and colors exploded around us, all we could do
was marvel in the majesty of the moment.

Was this a dream?

Was it a vision of heaven?

Had I been transported into some other realm where I was beholding mysteries usually hidden from mortals?

No...we were on the National Mall in Washington, D.C., and it was America's 230th Fourth of July celebration. The diversity of the hundreds of thousands of people gathered for the occasion underscored what a melting pot America really is. We were standing at the base of the Washington Monument and from there we could see the Lincoln Memorial, the Jefferson Memorial, the Capitol, and the White House. The flood of light on each of the structures caused them to gleam in the summer night. Not too far away the Potomac River was flowing. Several hours of entertainment by musicians from multiple genres extolled the virtues of American democracy. And by the time the crowd dismissed, the sky had flashed and boomed nonstop for nearly a half hour with a matchless display of fireworks, all in a grand celebration of liberty.

As memorable as this event was, even in the midst of it I found my thoughts wandering—not wandering aimlessly, mind you, but wandering nonetheless. Wandering to a day yet to come, wandering to an experience that some we love have already begun to enjoy, wandering to another place. I'm speaking of heaven, where God will be worshiped for eternity by everyone who in this life places his or her faith in Christ.

Worship—recognizing and ascribing to God His proper worth and lovingly giving Him the adoration He's due—is, after all, the agenda of heaven. And it was the worship of God in heaven that the apostle John was allowed to glimpse late in his life while he was in exile for his faith on the island of Patmos, off the coast of Greece. The last book of the Bible, commonly called the Revelation, records his experience. There he says,

> I, John, your brother and fellow partaker in the tribula-
> tion and kingdom and perseverance which are in Jesus,

was on the island called Patmos because of the word of God and the testimony of Jesus. I was in the Spirit on the Lord's day, and I heard behind me a loud voice like the sound of a trumpet, saying, "Write in a book what you see" (Revelation 1:9-11).

What he saw, among other things, included this enthralling scene:

I looked, and behold, a door standing open in heaven, and the first voice which I had heard, like the sound of a trumpet speaking with me, said, "Come up here, and I will show you what must take place after these things." Immediately I was in the Spirit; and behold, a throne was standing in heaven, and One sitting on the throne. And He who was sitting was like a jasper stone and a sardius in appearance; and there was a rainbow around the throne, like an emerald in appearance. Around the throne were twenty-four thrones; and upon the thrones I saw twenty-four elders sitting, clothed in white garments, and golden crowns on their heads. Out from the throne come flashes of lightning and sounds and peals of thunder.

And before the throne there was something like a sea of glass, like crystal; and in the center and around the throne, four living creatures full of eyes in front and behind. The first creature was like a lion, and the second creature like a calf, and the third creature had a face like that of a man, and the fourth creature was like a flying eagle. And the four living creatures, each one of them having six wings, are full of eyes around and within; and day and night they do not cease to say, "Holy, holy, holy is the Lord God, the Almighty, who was and who is and who is to come."

And when the living creatures give glory and honor and thanks to Him who sits on the throne, to Him who lives forever and ever, the twenty-four elders will fall down before Him who sits on the throne, and will worship

Him who lives forever and ever, and will cast their crowns before the throne, saying, "Worthy are You, our Lord and our God, to receive glory and honor and power; for You created all things, and because of Your will they existed, and were created" (Revelation 4:1-11).

As this scene continued to unfold, John "saw between the throne (with the four living creatures) and the elders a Lamb standing, as if slain.... the four living creatures and the twenty-four elders fell down before the Lamb.... And they sang a new song, saying, 'Worthy are You...for You were slain, and purchased for God with Your blood men from every tribe and tongue and people and nation'" (Revelation 5:6,8-9).

John then "heard the voice of many angels...and the number of them was myriads of myriads, and thousands of thousands, saying with a loud voice, 'Worthy is the Lamb that was slain to receive power and riches and wisdom and might and honor and glory and blessing'" (Revelation 5:12).

What John was seeing, and what the Bible spells out even more fully, was the culmination of the story that God began unfolding even before the foundation of the world—the story that He has been working to bring to pass ever since.

It's the story of the One who accomplished God's desire to offer men and women freedom from their sins, the One who vanquishes every foe of this glorious liberty, the One who said, "If the Son makes you free, you will be free indeed" (John 8:36).

I'm personally glad that, because of God's grace, I have become not only a citizen of this wonderful country in which I was born, but also a citizen of heaven through the new birth He gives those who trust in Christ. I'm increasingly filled with anticipation at the unending celebration of His greatness that awaits when I arrive there.

Certainly, even now, I know the truth of the apostle Peter's words when he wrote, "Though you have not seen Him, you love Him, and though you do not see Him now, but believe in Him, you greatly rejoice with joy inexpressible and full of glory" (1 Peter 1:8).

Still, though, when that day comes, I'm looking forward to being able to worship and give thanks to Him for His forgiveness and freedom, and for who He is, without the hindrances of my own humanity or of this passing world. That's going to be some kind of celebration.

It's what you and I were made for.

Let the festivities begin!

Draw Near and Be Transformed

History is the story of the One who is "the Alpha and the Omega, the beginning and the end" (Revelation 21:6). It's all about the One who makes it possible for people like you and me to dwell forever by the "river of the water of life, clear as crystal, coming from the throne of God and of the Lamb" (Revelation 22:1).

As surely as rivers flow to the sea, you and I are powerless to alter that course. However, we can choose to be part of it by placing our faith in the Lord Jesus Christ.

So the question now is the same as it has always been: Will you draw near to Him and be transformed? And in belonging to Him, will you make yourself available for Him to use in helping others experience His saving love?

Yes? Great…then let's get on with it.

A Final Word

It has not appeared as yet what we will be.
We know that when He appears, we will be like Him,
because we will see Him just as He is.

1 John 3:2

> Those whose well-being is limited
> by what they can figure out will never,
> this side of heaven, be well.

What I have written in the preceding pages is not mere theory.

To be sure, it does represent doctrine, or what I believe based on the unique, supremely reliable insight into God's nature and purpose that He has given us in His Word, the Bible.

But what I have written is also what I am experiencing and proving true in the refining fire of my life. Life, after all, has a way of testing opinion, theory, doctrine, and everything else. Sooner or later in life, reality presses in upon us in ways that shake us to the core and either validate our assumptions or shred them. For those who believe aright, even humanly tragic circumstances can become the backdrop against which divinely wonderful things can happen and the goodness of God can shine.

The Lord Jesus emphasized this truth as He concluded what's known as His Sermon on the Mount, which is recorded in the first book of the New Testament, the Gospel according to Matthew, chapters 5 through 7. At the end of the sermon, Jesus proclaimed,

> Everyone who hears these words of Mine and acts on them, may be compared to a wise man who built his house on the rock. And the rain fell, and the floods came, and the winds blew and slammed against that house; and yet it did not fall, for it had been founded on the rock. Everyone who hears these words of Mine and does not act on them, will be like a foolish man who built his house on the sand. The rain fell, and the floods came, and the winds blew and slammed against that house; and it fell—and great was its fall (verses 24-27).

A few days after the personal tragedy I've related in the course of this book, I sat on our patio in Charlotte under a mild Carolina winter sky reflecting on the stunning blur of sorrow that had so swiftly befallen us, like some giant meteor crashing down on our world from outer space. I did not presume to try to understand it all. Those whose well-being is limited by what they can figure out will never, this side of heaven, be well, "for now we see in a mirror dimly...now I know in part" (1 Corinthians 13:12).

Still, however, I found that my soul came to rest on a certain core of unshakable conviction. I summed it up this way for the many people who had loved us, prayed for us, and poured kindness upon kindness upon us:

> As the days ahead unfold, we believe that the Lord will enable us to share in greater detail how we have encountered Him as we have walked through the valley of the shadow of death. For now, though, even as we continue to wade through deep waters which He has promised will not overflow us, please hear and share this message from us widely:

Jesus is enough.
Jesus is the only One who is enough.
In fact, Jesus is more than enough.

Simply put, that is the message of this book. My prayer is that the exchange we've had through these pages will help you draw near to Him and be transformed, so that you come to the place where you can say with us and countless others through history, "We know whom we have believed and are persuaded that He is able to keep what we have committed to Him until that day" (paraphrase of 2 Timothy 1:12).

Knowing Him is, after all, what true life is all about. One of my favorite songs[25] sums up life as a process that involves coming to Jesus for forgiveness, singing to Him out of gratitude, falling on Him as part of learning to walk with Him, crying to Him when things get tough, and dancing to Him as a result of the fullness He gives. I've written as one who, to this point in my relationship with Christ, has indeed done all those things. But for me the process isn't yet complete—eventually, I'll fully see Him as He is and be like Him.

For now, though, as my time in this world increasingly whitens my hair and etches my face with lines, I'm going to go on being captivated by Him and discovering more and more of the wonders of His goodness. Then one day, perhaps before too long, I'll finally get to—in the words of the song, "fly to Jesus" and "laugh on Glory's side."

That's going to be a great day. I hope you'll join me.

A TRIBUTE

to the Presence and Work of

THE LORD JESUS CHRIST

in the Life of

Nathan Thomas Parrish

NOVEMBER 17, 1980–JANUARY 24, 2006

He who once wandered in the far country
now worships in the heavenly country.

It's still hard to grasp that, after so few birthday celebrations, Nathan suddenly departed this world for his eternal home in the presence of Christ. Our grief is always there—just beneath the surface, ready to break through at any moment—and it's something that we're learning to "wear" through all the subsequent situations of life. As someone who has also faced great sorrow expressed it, "We now know terminal sadness. Always on the fringe of a laugh, there is a remembrance. And while we do not doubt that he's in the best place, we do so miss his face, and will for the rest of our lives."

Born with extraordinary spiritual sensitivity and trained up "in the way he should go" (Proverbs 22:6), Nathan was nonetheless lured for a while into a parched land of pleasures that pass. As his parents we prayed and, as it were, peered through the window many days (and many long nights) to catch a glimpse of him returning home.

At times we despaired that we might never see his familiar figure coming over the horizon toward us, or more accurately, toward the One we serve, whose promises never fail and who delights to show mercy and shower grace upon all who cast themselves upon Him.

Yet He—the Lord Jesus Christ—eventually had the last word in Nathan's life. Like the prodigal son of old (Luke 15:11-24), Nathan finally came to his senses and returned to his heavenly Father. He who once wandered in the far country—but who repented of his sins and came to walk with Christ, especially over the last two years of his life—now worships in the heavenly country.

Though the Lord took Nathan sooner than any of us expected, when He came for him He found Nathan about his heavenly Father's business. Vocationally, after graduating from college, he devoted himself as a camp instructor to helping kids experience the wonder of God's creation. He, too, reveled in it but, more important, he exulted in his relationship with the One who made it all, Christ. He also became a fearless witness—courageous like the Old Testament prophet bearing his same name—for the Savior who had changed his heart and life.

Since his death, one central truth has emerged: As Nathan completed his time here, he had become a loving and a relentless representative of his Redeemer. Just weeks before he died, he wrote, "It's been a really good year for me in many aspects: in my work, in my faith and vision of ministry.... I give all the glory to the good God we serve and pray that He will continue to bless me as I seek to honor Him in the mission field of this world."

The fact is, Nathan wanted everyone to know about the forgiveness and salvation Christ freely offers to all who come to Him in faith. "Jesus loves you; I love you" became his refrain. We have been thrilled to learn of individuals who have decided to trust Christ in response to Nathan's testimony. As one friend expressed it, "Nathan's path led to the cross and, even now, the 'trail markers' he left behind are continuing to point untold others in the same direction."

Helping youth point others to the cross of Christ is at the heart of the Billy Graham Evangelistic Association (BGEA) "Dare to be a Daniel" program. Targeted especially to adolescents, it brings them face to face with the principles of godliness embodied in the life of the Old Testament prophet Daniel, then teaches and helps them to stand for Christ and call others to faith in Him. God is using "Dare to be a Daniel" to raise up a generation of young people who know and serve the Lord with passion and boldness.

We, Nathan's loving family, don't know of a more fitting way to celebrate the Lord's presence and work in his life than by helping to extend "Dare to be a Daniel." Since January 24, 2006, many friends have contributed financially to BGEA as a tribute to Nathan and in order to help the program go forward. Many young people we know have participated in it and become evangelists in their families, schools, and communities. We invite you, too, to become involved in "Dare to be a Daniel" as God leads you, realizing that there is an eternal urgency about encouraging young people to walk with Christ.

For more information contact:

"Dare to be a Daniel"
P.O. Box 1290
Charlotte, NC 28201-1290
(Remember to mention Nathan Parrish)

On the Internet, visit www.daretobeadaniel.com

Phone 1-888-802-D2BD (1-888-802-3223)
toll-free 24 hours a day, 7 days a week

To contact Preston Parrish directly,
visit www.prestonparrish.com.

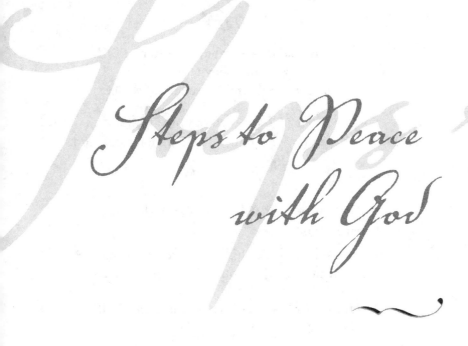

Steps to Peace with God

God loves you and wants you to experience peace and life abundant and eternal.

The Bible says...

- "we have peace with God through our Lord Jesus Christ" (Romans 5:1).

- "God so loved [your name] that He gave His only begotten Son," that [if you] believe in Him you "shall not perish, but have eternal life" (John 3:16).

- "I came that they may have life, and have it abundantly" (John 10:10).

**Since God planned for us to have peace and
the abundant life right now,
why are most people not having this experience?**

**God created us in His own image to have
an abundant life.**

**He did not make us as robots to automatically
love and obey Him,
but gave us a will and a freedom of choice.**

We chose to disobey God and go our own willful way. We still
make this choice today. This results in separation from God.

The Bible says...

- "All have sinned and fall short of the glory of God"
  (Romans 3:23).

- "The wages of sin is death, but the free gift of God is
  eternal life in Christ Jesus our Lord" (Romans 6:23).

Our choice results in separation from God.

Our Attempts

Through the ages, individuals have tried in many ways to bridge
this gap between themselves and God—through good works, religion, philosophy, morality—without success.

The Bible says...

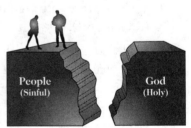

- "There is a way which seems
  right to man, but its end is
  the way of death" (Proverbs
  14:12).

- "Your iniquities have made
  a separation between you and your God, and your sins
  have hidden His face from you so that He does not hear"
  (Isaiah 59:2).

**There is only one remedy for this problem of separation.
Jesus Christ is the only answer to this problem.
He died on the cross and rose from the grave,
paying the penalty for our sin and**

bridging the gap between God and people.

The Bible says...

- "There is one God, and one mediator also between God and men, the man Christ Jesus" (1 Timothy 2:5).
- "Christ also died for sins once for all, the just for the unjust, so that He might bring us to God" (1 Peter 3:18).
- "God demonstrates His own love toward us, in that while we were yet sinners, Christ died for us" (Romans 5:8).

God has provided the only way through Christ. We must make the choice.

God provided us His Son, Jesus, who bridged the gap between sinful people and a holy God.

We must trust Jesus Christ and receive Him by personal invitation.

The Bible says...

- "Behold, I stand at the door and knock; if anyone hears My voice and opens the door, I will come in to him and will dine with him, and he with Me" (Revelation 3:20).
- "As many as received Him, to them He gave the right to become children of God, even to those who believe in His name" (John 1:12).
- "If you confess with your mouth Jesus as Lord, and believe in your heart that God raised Him from the dead, you will be saved" (Romans 10:9).

How to Receive Christ

- Admit your need (I am a sinner).

- Be willing to turn from your sins (repent).

- Believe that Jesus Christ died for you on the cross and rose from the grave.

- Through prayer, invite Jesus Christ to come in and control your life through the Holy Spirit (receive Him as Lord and Savior).

What to Pray

Dear Lord Jesus,

I know that I am a sinner and that I need Your forgiveness. I believe that You died for my sins. I want to turn from my sins. I now invite You to come into my heart and life. I want to trust and follow You as Lord and Savior.

In Jesus' name. Amen.

Scripture tells us that "whoever will call upon the name of the Lord will be saved" (Romans 10:13). Did you sincerely ask Jesus Christ to come into your life? Where is He right now? What has He given you?

The Bible Says…

- "By grace you have been saved, through faith; and that not of yourselves, it is the gift of God; not as a result of works, so that no one may boast" (Ephesians 2:8-9).

- "He who has the Son has life; he who does not have the Son of God does not have life. These things I have written to you who believe in the name of the Son of God, that you may know that you have eternal life, and that you may continue to believe in the name of the Son of God" (1 John 5:12-13 NKJV).

Receiving Christ, we are born into God's family through the

supernatural work of the Holy Spirit, who indwells every believer. This is called *regeneration*, or the new birth.

This is just the beginning of a wonderful new life in Christ. To deepen this relationship you should:

- Read your Bible every day to get to know Christ better.
- Talk to God in prayer every day.
- Tell others about Christ.
- Worship, fellowship, and serve with other Christians in a church where Christ is preached.
- As Christ's representative in a needy world, demonstrate your new life by your love and concern for others.

God bless you as you do.

For more information, contact:

Billy Graham Evangelistic Association
1 Billy Graham Parkway
Charlotte, NC 28201

Phone 1-877-2GRAHAM (1-877-247-2426)
toll-free 24 hours a day, 7 days a week

On the Internet, you can visit www.billygraham.org

End Notes

1. B.B. Warfield, as cited in Walter Elwell, *Evangelical Dictionary of Theology* (Grand Rapids, MI: Baker Book House Company, 1984), s.v. Only Begotten.

2. Suggested by domestic diva Dana Vines.

3. James I. Packer, *Knowing God* (Downers Grove, IL: InterVarsity Press, 1973), p. 185.

4. I know of no reason to conclude that Napoleon was acting in the spirit of the sixteenth century Protestant Reformers, who rejected the conventions of man-made religion and called people back to the authority of the Scriptures and to the foundational doctrine of salvation through faith in Christ alone. That would have been commendable on his part. As someone has said, "Religion is what sinful people try to do for a holy God. The Gospel is what holy God has already done for sinful people." Mere human religion, by any label, is futile.

5. For additional resources on this topic and others related to the basis for the Christian faith, you'll find books by premiere apologist Dr. Norman L. Geisler very helpful. They are available through local Christian bookstores and Internet booksellers. Also, contact AIIA Institute (Areopagus II America)—it's a fine ministry, directed by the Reverend Daryl Witmer, P.O. Box 262, Monson, Maine 04464. You can visit AIIA on the Internet at aiia.christiananswers.net or telephone them at 207-997-3644. Tell them Preston referred you, and request their free monthly "Thoughtletter"—it's excellent.

6. See Micah 5:2. God is more precise than even the latest global positioning system (GPS)—He not only knows the specific locations for people and events, He knows them in *advance!*

7. Suggested by legendary outdoorsman Charles A. Tope.

8. Suggested by undersea explorer David Green.

9. Suggested by noted scholar S. Max Scholle.

10. C.S. Lewis as cited at www.quotedb.com/quotes/346.

11. Biblical passages relating to this topic include Isaiah 14:12, Ezekiel 28:12-15, and Luke 10:18. While not explaining Satan comprehensively, these and other portions of Scripture tell us everything we need to know about him in this life. It's far more important to focus on understanding and experiencing everything we can about Christ the Savior rather than becoming preoccupied and sidetracked with questions about the devil, who is the ultimate loser.

12. Billy Graham, *Just As I Am: The Autobiography of Billy Graham* (Scranton, PA: HarperCollins, 1997), p. 139.

13. Billy Graham, *The Journey: How to Live by Faith in an Uncertain World* (Nashville: W Publishing Group, 2006) p. 109.

14. Lt. Col. Greer E. Noonburg, MD, as cited by Carolyn Rogers, "Orthopaedists Serve in Iraq," *Bulletin of the American Academy of Orthopedic Surgeons,* February 2004.

15. For more information about how to have an impact for Christ among inmates and their families, contact the organization founded by Charles Colson: Prison Fellowship, 44180 Riverside Parkway, Lansdowne, VA 20176, telephone 1-877-478-0100. You can visit them on the Internet at www.pfm.org.

16. *Journal of the American Medical Association (JAMA),* March 21, 1986.

17. This chapter is adapted from an article by Preston Parrish that originally appeared in *Decision* magazine, October 2004. Contact BGEA for a free trial subscription to *Decision,* which contains articles that will help you grow spiritually as well as exciting reports of what God is doing around the world.

18. In case the connection isn't apparent, the "Ellis" referred to at the opening of chapter 22, who comforted the coworker whose son died in a rock climbing fall, was indeed my father, Bruce Ellis Parrish Sr. He didn't dream then what would later happen with his grandson Nathan, who was only three at the time.

19. As cited at www.studylight.org/enc/isb/view.cgi?number=t7389.

20. See Josh McDowell's classic book *Evidence That Demands a Verdict* (Nashville: Thomas Nelson Publishers, 1993).

21. Excerpted from "Thine Be the Glory," written by Edmund Budry (1854–1932).

22. I have refrained from being overly specific or insistent about the sequence of events surrounding the Lord's return in an effort to maintain this book's essential focus on His person.

23. See Ephesians 5:25 and Revelation 19:7. I've now had the joy of witnessing the beauty and power of the relationship between Christ and His church pictured by two brides in our family—Glenda, when we wed, and our daughter Hannah, when she married Max. By the way, as this book was going to print, we received word that our first grandchild is on the way! "Blessed be the name of the LORD" (Job 1:21).

24. For more on this subject, see Franklin Graham's book *The Name* (Nashville: Thomas Nelson Publishers, 2002).

25. The song referred to here is "Untitled Hymn" by Chris Rice (©2003 Clumsy Fly Music, admin. by Word Music, Inc.).